In the "Preface of Saints" of our Mass, we give thanks to God for showing us his love, "enriching his Church with forms that are ever new and of admirable holiness."

These constantly renewed forms for encountering God are the schools of spirituality.

The richness of the Gospel is so great, and we are so limited that we cannot understand or live all of its aspects. Every Christian understands and lives certain facets of the mystery of Christ, and this partial living of the Christian truth constitutes the individual and unique spirituality of each believer.

But when this personal religious experience is converted into a model of living for many and is approved by the Church, "a school of spirituality" emerges.

Knowing a certain spirituality well is like learning a language to better communicate with God. There is no language superior to another. But God's providence assigns to each person a language uniquely his/her own.

In the same manner, there is no spirituality better than another, but there is one that, owing to God's providence, we should know and practice to a greater degree and more exactly.

This book is for those whom the Lord invites to live the Spirituality of the Cross, which we can also call the Spirituality of Christ the Priest.

The spring from which this new river emerged was the life and the writings of the Venerable Concepción Cabrera de Armida. And even though the Church has not yet canonized her, the spirituality itself has already been approved, through the Church's official approval of two religious congregations, two associations for the laity and one for priests, which are now living and spreading this spirituality.[1]

---

[1] Translator's note: These five aforementioned congregations and associations are known as the Works of the Cross. Many other congregations have sprung forth from this source and share the same spirituality. Along with the five original Works of the Cross, they comprise the Family of the Cross.

Ricardo Zimbrón Levy, M.Sp.S.

Priestly People

Nihil obstat
Edmundo de los Santos, M.Sp.S.

Imprimatur
Miguel Mier Maza, M.Sp.S.
March 2011

Original Spanish title *Pueblo Sacerdotal*,
by Ricardo Zimbrón Levy, M.Sp.S.
D.R. © Editorial La Cruz, S.A. de C.V.
San Luis Potosí 155, Col Roma, C.P. 06700
Mexico, D.F.

Translated by: Mary McCandless

Edited by: Elzbieta Sadowska, RCSCJ
          Martha Banner - Covenant of Love, Modesto CA
          Lynne Taliaferro - Covenant of Love, Modesto CA

TABLE OF CONTENTS

PART ONE

HISTORICAL BACKGROUND
OF THE SPIRITUALITY OF THE CROSS

FIRST PERIOD

1862 - 1893

First of all, we are going to examine the life of Mrs. Concepción Cabrera de Armida because she is, as we said, the origin and source of the spiritual current that we have set out to study.

We shall call her "Conchita" as everyone called her, especially her friends.

She was born on December 8, 1862, in San Luis Potosí, Mexico. Her parents were Octaviano Cabrera and Clara Arias. They had twelve children; Conchita was the seventh.

Her education was very brief and irregular because she spent her childhood in various *haciendas* belonging to her grandparents and lived in the city San Luis Potosí only for short periods of time. She related that as a child she studied first with the "elderly ladies of Santillán" and later with "Mrs. Negrete." She then studied six months with the Sisters of Charity. Finally, her mother obtained for her daughters various teachers, who gave them classes in the primary grades, as well as classes in embroidery and music. That was all. For that reason, she recorded with sincerity in her diary: "Regarding my instruction, it has been very meager."

Before continuing with her life story, I would like to point out how her extraordinary gift as a writer and teacher of the spiritual life contrasts with her "meager education."

In obedience to her spiritual directors she wrote her *Account of Conscience,* which is her spiritual diary covering many years. The original manuscript spans 66 notebooks. It begins in October 1893, and ends on December 8, 1936. Conchita died on March 3, 1937.

The copy of these writings, which I have in front of me, consists of 16 volumes, totaling 8,809 letter-sized pages, typed on a manual typewriter in single line spacing.

In addition, there are 10 notebooks of her autobiography, which she was required to write by Archbishop of Puebla, Ramón Ibarra, in order that they be sent to Rome for the purpose of "examining her spirit." There are several copies of this manuscript in existence.

Unless otherwise indicated, all of Conchita's quotations that are cited in this book come from these writings.

Additionally, Conchita wrote 44 booklets that have been published. Several are still in print today.

In the process of the cause for canonization of this servant of God, other writings that had been dispersed were collected: many letters to family members, to priests and bishops, some narratives, unedited treatises, prayers and advice to individuals and communities. All of this material comprises 102 volumes of manuscripts, which are kept in the archives of the Missionaries of the Holy Spirit.

In Conchita's writings, we frequently find expressions such as "The Lord spoke to me...," "The Lord told me...," "The Lord made me see...," or "I saw Jesus and He told me to write...."

Conchita, indeed, had the charism of prophecy, the charism preferred by St. Paul that consists of receiving messages directly from God through spoken words or visions.

This explains how Conchita, despite her lack of education, wrote innumerable pages that would have been difficult to write, even for a doctor of theology. All of these writings constitute the primary fount of the Spirituality of the Cross.

But now, we will continue with our history.

Conchita recalled many experiences from her childhood, among them her first confession. She was eight years old and she was in the convent school of the Sisters of Charity. Since she didn't know what to say to her confessor, she asked one of the older children, and this child told Conchita some very grave sins for her to confess. Conchita memorized these sins and told them to the priest, even though she did not understand what she was saying. The priest looked out of the confessional to see who was speaking, and upon seeing such a small child with such grave sins, he scolded her severely and gave her 15 rosaries as penance.

She remembered yet another confession:

"My confessor asked me: 'Are you married?'

"'No,' I answered.

"'Are you a maiden?'

"'No Father,' again I responded, because to me, maidens were like the maidens of honor of certain very elegant women.

"'Well, then, what are you?' the priest said rather roughly.

"'Well, what am I, dear Lord?' I thought.

"'I...am Conchita Cabrera,' I answered him, because I could not think of any other response. God forgive me such foolishness!"

Reminiscing on her First Holy Communion, which occurred when she was ten years old, Conchita wrote:

"I don't remember anything in particular about this day because of my tepidity and lack of comprehension, just an immense interior joy and great pleasure because of my white dress. But from that day on, my love for the Eucharist began to grow. After that, I was always greatly pleased to receive the most Blessed Sacrament. It became an indispensable need in my life."

And she remembered something else:

"Even in those early years, I felt a strong inclination to prayer, penance, and above all to purity.

"I spent long hours on the flat roof of my house contemplating heaven and wished I could penetrate it with my heart. It was a thirst for something very big with which to fill my poor soul, a thirst that longed for the Supreme Good.

"Nature and music have always drawn me to God. Almost without my even knowing it, Lord, I felt your presence, your beauty, your power and goodness within me. But I was very bad and I quickly forgot you and tossed those sentiments, those interior touches of the Holy Spirit, on the ground. I lived an animal-like life, concerned only for external things, without virtues and without fruits for heaven.

"I continued to grow up this way, naturally, like a wild weed. And how poorly I understood, my God, your graces and favors – and that unique predilection with which you always covered my unworthy soul."

On Conchita's thirteenth birthday, she was taken to her first formal dance. There she met a young man named Francisco Armida, who would eventually become her husband. And a month later, at another dance, her engagement was formalized.

"I have to thank Pancho, who never took advantage of my innocence. He was a very proper and respectful suitor.

"For me, my engagement did not interfere with my surrender to God. It was so easy to do both things. I went to bed thinking of Pancho, but later, before falling asleep, I would think of the Eucharist, which was my delight.

"From the age of 16 to 20, I passed through an era of dances, theaters, promenades, vanities and a great desire to please, although only to please Pancho, for other men did not attract me.

"In the midst of this sea of vanities and festivities, my soul felt a vehement desire to learn how to pray. I would ask others, I would read and however I could, I would try to place myself in the presence of God. Then I would receive much enlightenment about the nothingness of worldly things, the vanity of life, the beauty of God and I felt a great love for the Holy Spirit. When I would go to bed, I would take my crucifix and I don't know what came over me as I contemplated it: a profound inner turmoil, a nailing of the heart upon that cross, something impossible to explain.

"But this impression would pass and I would return to my ordinary life of tepidity, vanity and foolishness."

During this time, Conchita lived in a property belonging to her mother, the *"Peregrina"* [Pilgrim] hacienda. She learned to milk cows, make cheese and bread, mount a horse and teach the little girls of the hired help how to read. She related that her mother taught her how to cook all sorts of dishes and also showed her how to manage the household.

"This was a beautiful and peaceful life, but I was concerned about Pancho, who was in San Luis. Sometimes I would take out his picture so he could see the beautiful nature. How simple and foolish I have always been!"

Finally, when she was going to be 22 years of age, as was the custom of the time, the Canon priest, Francisco Peña, presented himself to Conchita's parents to ask for their daughter's hand in marriage, on behalf of Pancho Armida. After almost nine years of courtship, Conchita was married on November 8, 1884, in Our Lady of Carmel Church, the crown architectural jewel of San Luis Potosí.

Remembering her husband, Conchita wrote the following: "He was a good man: a Christian, a gentleman, honorable, proper, intelligent, and with a big heart. He was sensitive to any misfortune, as well as charitable, and tender and loving with me, and an excellent father. He had no concerns except to care for his children. They were his joy and he suffered much whenever they were ill.

"When we got married, he had an explosive nature. But he was like gunpowder; once the fire had passed, he would become content and repentant for what he had done. But after a few years, he changed so much that his mother and his siblings were amazed. I think it was the grace of God, and Pancho's constant smoothing out of the rough edges of his character by means of this sandpaper that I am for him.

"He was very much afraid of death. Whenever I read the *Imitation of Christ* to him, the subject of death came up frequently and he thought that I read this on purpose.

"When I became gravely ill, which happened several times, he would always stay at my side day and night.

"He was a little jealous and very particular about his appearance. But when he was near death, he asked me to dress him in an old Franciscan habit and to bury him in a second-class lot.

"Before dying, he made his general confession and his fear of dying changed into a tranquil abandonment to the will of God. He told me, 'It seems to me that this is when the children need me the most, but God knows what he is doing and I only wish to do his will.'"

Conchita was married for 17 years and had 9 children. She perfectly fulfilled her role as wife and mother and loved with great affection the man whom God had given her as her spouse.

Nevertheless, she discovered after a few years of marriage, that her true happiness would have been in a total consecration to God in the religious life. She never showed this externally. She shared this solely with her spiritual director and wrote this in her diary:

"When I met the nuns of the Sacred Heart, I felt a holy envy in my soul, so much so that I became teary-eyed whenever I approached that chapel. Only Jesus could see the pain in my heart, realizing that I could not consecrate myself to him.

"An altered vocation, whether one's own fault or not, is one of the worst martyrdoms there is.

"Oh my Jesus, if only I could live solely for you! Then I would be truly happy."

The birth of their first son filled the young couple with great joy. He was born on September 28, 1885, and they named him Francisco. Conchita remembered: "I offered him to the Lord with all my heart. After the child was born, his father got down on his knees, sobbing and giving thanks to God."

Then came a very important page in her diary, because it signaled a new period in her spiritual life:

"After a year and a half of marriage (May of 1886), the Lord began to call me even more forcefully to perfection. From then on, extraordinary things began to happen."

The "extraordinary things that began to happen", to which Conchita refers, were two short visions of Jesus, and above all, the experience of the presence of God, filling her and possessing her:

"Today I do not know what to write. I wouldn't be able to anyway. Such are the things that my soul is experiencing. Oh my God, you have taken possession of me so completely that I think I cannot even move without your willing it. I am no longer in control of the powers of my soul or anything else. You have filled me completely. Oh my Jesus, why don't you just yank out my soul once and for all and take it with you? Oh my! You just rouse it, and then you leave it to suffer. I do not know what you want from me, but I am ready for anything. You see, I cannot endure this extraordinary sensation. My spiritual side gains much, but my body feels like it is dying. The truth is, I do not know what is happening to me. All I know is that my heart is aching."

This invasion of Conchita's soul and life continued for three years. Then, on August 28, 1889, while she was doing her first spiritual exercises, Our Lord showed her for the first time what her mission was to be: "One day, a day when I put myself completely at the disposal of whatever God wanted from me, at the moment when the Father spoke to me, I heard very clearly, within the very depths of my soul and without a doubt, these words which astounded me: YOUR MISSION IS TO SAVE SOULS. I could not understand how this could be. It struck me as so strange and impossible."

At another time, she related her most intimate thoughts on this: "Me, save souls, Lord? But as you can see, I can barely save my own."

A few days after these spiritual exercises, Conchita spent some time at the *Jesús María* hacienda, the property of her brother Octaviano. With her were the three children she had at that time: Francisco, Carlos, and Manuel. While there, Conchita had this experience:

"Today I was saying my prayers under the trees in the garden, when I felt the desire to invite my Lord to accompany me. He deigned to hear me, because I felt his presence next to me. I began to talk to him and I felt that he gave me the following counsel: That, with much confidence, I should always call upon him, so he could show me how to walk in his presence throughout the entire day. That from the morning on, I should invite him like a good friend and be attentive to him as such, to talk with him and to take him to all my daily activities.

"Later, he left, and I remained with an emptiness that could not be filled. The next day I called him again and that's how it was for a long time; each time he would come.

"But many times I would abandon him and my fickle mind would concern itself with foolishness. Forgive me, adorable Jesus! May the day come very soon when we will never again be separated."

On September 29th, 1890, Conchita gave birth to a baby girl, who was named María Concepción.

That year she wrote to her confessor, the Canon Francisco Peña:

"I have felt a serious and profound transformation. At times I feel called to a quietude, to a form of prayer that does not depend on me. Without thinking, without reading, without coming up with my own ideas, my heart begins to dilate in a manner that I cannot explain. It is an inexplicable happiness. I believe that this is how it must feel in heaven, because it is only the spirit that is overjoyed. But not of its own accord, or when I wish it, but rather, it is a special gift from God."

It can be clearly seen how Conchita was entering into the mystical life, in which individuals are purely passive in their religious experiences. It is God who works mightily in them.

After experiencing so many favors from our Lord, Conchita reviewed her feelings in this manner:

"May vanity never enter my mind, not even for a moment. These are treasures from Jesus. These are such immense favors, that due to their own grandeur, they make me hesitate, because I understand my nothingness.

"But if God is so kind to his enemies, how would it be for his friends? And if Jesus wanted to descend to a humble manger, why would he not want to come to my poor self? I think that if Jesus does such favors for the holy souls, he would also do the same for the ones who are in need and miserable, because his generosity is limitless."

But let us not think that Conchita's life was all filled with spiritual consolations and outward prosperity. God always purifies and perfects his chosen ones through the cross.

On March 10, 1893, her son Carlitos died at the age of six. The cause was typhoid fever, which in those days was very often fatal.

Four months after the death of her son, Conchita wrote:

"The time for testing is now occurring. It has been a raw and very difficult experience for my weakened state of being. First, I had spiritual struggles, then economic difficulties and desolation. And

17

then - Oh my Jesus, you yanked my son from my arms, tearing my heart apart. You have transplanted him to heaven, leaving behind a wound in my soul that will never heal. Who could have told me that my son would see so soon what I have not yet seen, and have unveiled for him that which I myself cannot come to understand. I thank you for this blessed separation, but let me cry. Lord, gather these tears that do not spring from a rebellion against your holy will, but rather from this heart of flesh."

Because of everything that was happening to her, especially because of the extraordinary graces that she was receiving and her desire for holiness, Conchita felt the need for a spiritual director. "A great devotion to the Holy Spirit was born in me and I asked him for a director who could understand me."

On April 8, 1893, Conchita had her fifth child. She named him Ignacio.

A little later, a Jesuit priest who had arrived in San Luis agreed to guide her spiritually. His name was Alberto Cuscó y Mir. He was a holy and wise priest. He ordered Conchita to write her memoirs, that is, to record all that had happened up to that time; and also, at his instruction, she began to write daily her *Account of Conscience* which, as we stated, began in October of 1893.

Conchita wrote the following about Father Mir: "I have never seen a more incredulous priest in dealing with things of the spirit. He told me that he feels that everything is from God, but nevertheless he was going to 'keep me in quarantine.'"

Interestingly, their roles would later reverse themselves. Conchita began to doubt herself, thinking that everything was an illusion or fantasy. But now it was Father Mir who assured her to the contrary:

"Regarding your doubts, I tell you that I don't see anything that is not from God. Don't doubt this. Sometimes in minor or incidental issues you mix in some things of your own imagination, as I have told you before. But this is not important. The reality, truth, and substance are truly from God."

One excellent judgment of Father Mir was to realize the plan that God had for Conchita and to guide her toward that goal.

"Jesus destines every soul to a purpose and he gives that soul a charism for this destiny. He gave St. Francis de Sales patience and sweetness; he gave St. Ignatius a bellicose spirit; he gave St. Teresa of Avila an enterprising spirit. And he wants you for suffering and for love, saturated with suffering and saturated with love. This is the distinct character of your spirit. As is said of Christ, that he was a 'man of suffering,' you shall be, in as much as an earthly creature can be, a 'woman of suffering,' to imitate the Blessed Virgin Mary, herself so full of sorrow.

"It seems plain to me that you are destined for the cross. Don't think of anything but your crucified Jesus consumed in anguish, saturated with pain and wasted by desolation. This should be your way of thinking from here on and these should be your aspirations."

As we shall see, the words of Father Mir were very prophetic.

SECOND PERIOD

1894 - 1897

After having narrated the first period of Conchita's life from birth to age thirty-two, we are now going to describe a second period, short in its duration, but rich in its events.

We will now explore the year 1894. It was a very important year: On January 14th, in an act of intense love and generosity, she branded a monogram with the name of Jesus on her chest. With this she wanted to tell the Lord that she belonged to him – she was his property – for she had seen animals branded in a similar manner on the haciendas, marking them as property of their owners. Later, propelled by a great desire that all souls be saved, she repeated over and over: "Jesus Savior of men, save them!"

On January 23th, she made a "TOTAL SURRENDER" to Our Lord. She herself formulated the surrender and it was approved by her spiritual director. In response, Jesus gave her the grace of "spiritual betrothal." It is a grace of mystical order, the kind that St. John of the Cross and St. Teresa of Avila (the sixth mansion) spoke about. It consists of an extraordinary union between the Word made flesh and a soul, and it is a preparation for an even greater grace that the mystics call "spiritual marriage" or "transforming union."

Regarding the extraordinary event of January 23rd, Conchita wrote:

"I was submerged in deep contemplation, very still, understanding many things in great depth, listening to the words of Jesus. He was doing it all. He put his hand on my head; his gaze seemed to bathe me completely. And I, all I could do was weep unceasingly. What could I tell you since I could think of nothing else to do but annihilate myself? Jesus told me:

21

"'Now you are truly my spouse, and in my eyes you are beautiful, with a veil of innocence and a dress of penitence: I love you very much, and now I ask you to call me Spouse.'

"'Not that, Jesus, for I am embarrassed.'

"'Ask me anything you want; today I cannot deny you anything.'

"'I ask that I may always do your will and save many souls.'"

Conchita counted February 4th of that year as one of the happiest days of her life, because on that day she took perpetual vows of poverty, chastity according to her married state, and obedience to God and to all who represented him: her husband, her mother, her spiritual director, and her bishop.

In that same month of February, Conchita had a very important vision when she was at a church called *Iglesia de la Compania* in San Luis Potosí.

"I saw a great fire, like rays of light, almost white, very clear and brilliant, even more brilliant than electricity. In the center of this light was a very white dove with its wings extended and below it, in the depths of the immense light, was a large cross, very large, with a heart at its center. The heart had very sharp thorns that surrounded it and seemed to be pressing against it very tightly and even penetrating it. It hurt just to look at these thorns. There was a lance whose tip pierced the heart and made the blood pour out upon the cross.

"The heart was alive, not just painted. It was a pulsating human heart, made of flesh, and yet, at the same time, glorified. It was as though surrounded by a moving fire-like material, as if inside a fire pit, and on top, sprouting from its interior, another type of flame, like tongues of fire of greater intensity, distinct from the fire that surrounded the cross. These flames leapt about violently, like eruptions from a volcano, covering and then uncovering a smaller cross that was planted on the heart or maybe coming out from it.

"Without my willing it or expecting it, I began to experience visions of this cross multiple times. This lasted two months or more, to the point that it was not only during times of prayer, but other times as well; during the day, at night, whenever, even in the middle of my daily tasks, that cross would appear to me.

"'What is this?' I would ask myself. 'What does the Lord want?'"

We have said that this vision has great significance. Through it, God revealed a visual synthesis of a new school of spirituality to Conchita. This was the school of spirituality that he wanted to establish in his Church by means of five institutions that are now called the five "Works of the Cross," all of which have as an emblem the symbolic image of the cross which was revealed to Conchita.

In March, Conchita's sister, Clara, made the first drawing of this mysterious cross. And later, Margarito Vela, a painter from San Luis Potosí, made an oil painting of the cross.

"When I saw the finished painting, I was filled with an inexplicable joy, although it seemed to me that this was but a shadow of what I had seen, for one cross was just painted, whereas the other one had life. The painting was very good, except that the size of the cross is different, hardly comparable. And the light. . . ! I don't think there exist any colors that can reproduce that celestial clarity. But the painting gives a slight idea of that vision."

The image of this vision which Conchita described is now widespread in drawings, sculptures, medals and prints. It is called the "Cross of the Apostolate," because in the beginning it was the insignia of the "Apostleship of the Cross," the first of the five Works, and later, the symbol for the other four.

We are now going to explain the symbolism of this vision. Let us recall that it is a visual synthesis of the elements that constitute the spirituality based on the priesthood of Christ.

The large cross represents the external passion of Jesus; it is the altar upon which Christ the priest offered the holocaust of his body and blood to the Father. It is also the cross that we must carry if we want to be disciples of Jesus. "If a man wishes to come after me, he must deny his very self, take up his cross and follow me" (Mt 16:24).

It is our "daily cross" (cf. Lk 9:23), united with the Cross of Christ, which participates in its redemptive value and allows us to reach a very special intimacy with him.

But suffering of itself has no value: "If I hand over my body to be burned, but have not love, I gain nothing" (1Co 13:3). For that reason, the symbol of the Holy Spirit hovers over the Cross, the Spirit that filled the heart of Christ, the Spirit that enkindled in Christ his immense love for the Father and all mankind, and that moved him to offer himself as a victim to God to remove our sins: "Moved by the Holy Spirit, He offered himself as a spotless offering to God" (He 9:14).

The Holy Spirit is also the one who reveals the value of the Cross of Christ to us and leads us to embrace it. Without the light of the Holy Spirit, the Cross of Christ can only be considered as a "scandal and madness." Only with the grace of the Holy Spirit can we understand that "what seems to be a mark of weakness in God is stronger than all the strength of men and what seems to be the foolishness of God, is wiser than all the wisdom of men" (1Co 1:25).

The heart in the center of the Cross, embraced by flames, encircled by thorns and pierced by a lance, signifies the immense love of Christ for his Father and for us, which reached its maximum expression in his painful surrender "unto death, death on the Cross" (Phil 2:8).

The small cross, "planted upon the heart," symbolizes the interior sufferings of Christ, his pain over the lamentable situation of humankind who, because of sin, does not live in love. It symbolizes his sadness over the ingratitude and lack of comprehension of many souls, as well as his sorrow for being abandoned by his friends and for the infidelities of those who were associated most intimately with his work of salvation.

The light and the clouds symbolize the loving presence of the Father, whose love is the beginning and origin of the salvation of man, and who is pleased by the perfect surrender of the Son, who out of obedience gives his life as a ransom for all mankind.

Archbishop of Mexico Luis M. Martínez, who was Conchita's spiritual director for the last twelve years of her life, wrote these illuminating teachings:

"In the Cross of the Apostolate, one can find all the treasures that Jesus bequeathed to us. If we want to express this magnificent symbolism in words, we can use that passage from the letter to the Hebrews: 'through the Holy Spirit, Christ offered himself as an unblemished host to God'" (He 9:14).

Through the Holy Spirit, symbolized by the Dove, Jesus offered himself to the Father. He showed us his heart, immaculate and full of love. He offered himself to God the Father, who is represented in that vision by the "inaccessible light."

This cross expresses Jesus' priesthood in a graphic manner. Therefore, "in order to understand it and to comprehend our spirituality, we need to understand Jesus' priesthood."

"Jesus' priesthood has one beginning: LOVE. It has one essence: IMMOLATION; and it has one end: THE GLORY OF GOD AND THE SALVATION OF MEN."

The Holy Spirit is infinite love, eternal love, divine love, through which Jesus "offered himself to God as an unblemished host." The heart pierced by the lance, surrounded by thorns and embraced by flames is Jesus who, driven by that love, immolates himself. The celestial light is the Father, who accepts the sacrifice of the Son as the price for our redemption.

The priesthood of Jesus is the center of the Church, instituted to perpetuate his sacrifice and to distribute his fruits. It is the center of new life, it is the center of history and it is the center of the universe – because the only thing that satisfies the Father is the love of the Son, which manifests itself in his "obedience even unto death on the Cross." And all the joys that the Father encounters in his creatures, or the glory that he receives from them, are bound to the priesthood and the sacrifice of Christ.

If we want to live out the priesthood of Jesus, each one of us needs to be a personification of that mysterious cross – a living Cross of the Apostolate. We need to live each day offering ourselves to the Father, in union with Jesus, moved by that love which only the Holy Spirit can infuse into our hearts. This is the sum of our spirituality.

Now, throughout the following stages of Conchita's life, we will narrate the history of the five WORKS OF THE CROSS. These are of utmost importance in understanding what we are studying, given that its final goal is precisely to promulgate this doctrine and to give us the means to live it out. Through these five Works, Conchita's personal spirituality is converted into a true school of spirituality.

THE APOSTLESHIP OF THE CROSS is, chronologically, the first of the five works: "In February my spiritual director wrote to me and stated, 'You will save many souls, but through the apostolate of the cross.' He was referring to the fact that I, through my sacrifices, united with those of Our Lord, would save many souls. But upon reading that document, when I reached the part where it stated 'apostolate of the cross,' I cannot explain it, but I felt something grand, something extraordinary. I felt a world of light that made me see that not only could I be an apostle of the cross, but that thousands of souls could join me in being that, too. This was the origin of the Apostleship of the Cross."

On April 18, Conchita drew up the first rough draft of the statutes of this association, following the guidance of her spiritual director. Father Mir corrected these notes and Conchita rewrote them.

"I took the statutes of the Apostleship to Jesus so that he could bless them and give them life. And after Communion, he told me: 'The purpose of this Apostleship is to lovingly offer one's suffering so as to achieve the salvation of many souls.'"

These statutes have evolved with the passage of time, to be updated and adapted to current circumstances in the best possible manner. I will quote the following paragraphs from the current statutes to give us some idea of the nature of this work and the spirituality that it transmits:

The Apostleship of the Cross is a group of Christians who, moved by the Holy Spirit, have dedicated themselves to offering Jesus to the Celestial Father and to offering themselves, united with Christ, as victims for the salvation of all. In this manner they strive to participate intimately in the priesthood of Jesus, offering themselves together with him on the cross each day.

This work is for all Christians who seek to live out their baptismal priesthood, so that they can respond in this manner to the universal call to holiness.

The Apostleship of the Cross helps an individual discover the salvific value of sacrificial suffering, a suffering lived for the love of Christ and in union with Christ as Priest and Victim. The emphasis on the redemptive strength of the sacrifice of Christ propels one to live in the integrity of the Paschal mystery, the center of the Gospel and the culmination of human redemption.

Pain is an incomprehensible mystery for humankind, who instinctively rejects it. This mystery is illuminated only when it finds its meaning in Christ, who *was obedient even unto death on the Cross,'* in order to show his love for the Father and to save humanity.

Our suffering, united with that of Christ, is also an instrument of salvation. As such, it is a true apostolate.

The members of the Apostleship of the Cross participate with love in the sacrifice of Jesus for the sake of the entire Church, but especially for her priests, so that they can respond with fidelity to their vocation, a vocation to participate more fully in the priesthood of Jesus.

The author of our transformation into Jesus is the Holy Spirit. Only by being illumined and strengthened by the Spirit's graces can we embrace each day's cross with love and so transform it into a joyful offering to God.

The vocation to transform ourselves into Christ, Priest and Victim, can only be realized by means of a series of encounters with him, each time more intimate than the last, which leads us to have his very sentiments. For that reason, in our spirituality, frequent and persevering prayer is absolutely necessary.

Mary associated herself as a mother with the priestly offering of Christ through her loving acceptance of the Father's will and her consent to the immolation of the Victim whom she herself had engendered. Thus, she manifests herself as the most perfect model in offering Christ and us in union with him.

IN SUMMARY

The essence of our commitment consists in making an offering of Christ, Priest and Victim, in offering ourselves in union with him on our daily cross, and in identifying ourselves with the will of the Father in filial and loving obedience. This is all done through the action of the Holy Spirit, in union with the Blessed Virgin Mary.

According to the structure of the Apostleship of the Cross, this commitment can have two modes: fundamental or integral.

THE FUNDAMENTAL COMMITMENT CONSISTS OF:

—Living in grace, that is, without grievous sin.

—Offering Christ, Priest and Victim, and offering ourselves in union with him in the midst of our daily lives.

—Embracing the cross with love each day, starting with realizing perfectly the duties and obligations of our own state of life.

—Offering Sunday Mass and Communion for our priests and for vocations.

—Giving testimony to our faith, in accordance with our personal situation.

THE INTEGRAL COMMITMENT CONSISTS OF:

—The elements outlined previously and the following:

—Following the processes of formation put forth by the Apostleship in its Regulations.

—Having an organized apostolate according to individual circumstances.

—Participating in the community activities of the

organization: the meetings, the internal and apostolic activities of the "small group" or of the Central group to which one belongs.

As you can see, this Apostleship is for everyone and within reach of everyone. There may be many people who cannot make the Integral Commitment, but there is no one who cannot make the Fundamental Commitment. Truly living this commitment suffices to reach the holiness to which God calls us, through the path of this Apostleship.

Conchita was not someone who could have committed to very many meetings or activities. Her time was taken up with her pregnancies and the births of her nine children, amidst baby bottles and sleepless nights and as she put it, "amid sewing clothes, problems with servants, economic difficulties and family parties." She was a wife and a mother to many children of varying ages and with frequent illnesses. That is why she is the perfect secular model. She represents those who have much to do in this world. But just because they are busy does not mean that they are not invited to holiness. It is precisely by the offering up of their daily work, which is many times painful and full of suffering, that they progress in holiness.

I believe that the Apostleship of the Cross, through its flexibility, is called to gather a great multitude of people, always and whenever the directors take into consideration that the "Fundamental Commitment" is the most essential aspect of this endeavor and that this is enough to meet the goals of the Apostleship perfectly. Sometimes too great a preoccupation with institutionalization kills the spirit.

In this same year, 1894, Conchita received from our Lord the first ideas regarding the foundation of a religious community of women that would live according to the spirituality of Jesus, Priest and Victim. In one of her writings, which she entitled *History of the Sisters of the Cross*, we read the following:

"My director had given me a document so that I could meditate on some points in it. I was sitting on a pew somewhere in the middle of a church called the '*Templo de la Compañia,*' when I felt that the Lord was speaking to me. I was determined to ignore him, wanting to meditate on the document, but I couldn't. Finally, after asking him to help me remain faithful and to love him always, I suddenly received an internal vision of an immense procession of religious women with a large red cross on their backs. They were processing side by side and took a long time to pass me by. I was astonished and did not understand what this meant, so I remained silent. Suddenly I heard the voice of my Jesus, who told me: 'There shall be a congregation which shall be called the Oasis, because there is where my heart shall rest. And thus shall the religious women be who will form it.'

"He told me that after the Congregation of the Sisters of the Cross was approved, there would follow a congregation of religious men, his brothers and they, too, would be approved by the Church. Both congregations would give him much glory.

"Rarely during the next few years did he mention the congregation of religious men, and then only from time to time, regarding its mission and its founding. He spoke of it as something that would surely happen, and I halfheartedly believed it.

"On Holy Thursday in 1894, after I received Communion, he told me: 'Within a few years you will adore me at the Oasis on this memorable day, amidst many living crosses. This day will be a great feast for these women, given that one of the purposes of this congregation will be the adoration of the Eucharist.

"You will be the foundation of this congregation, a foundation that is not seen, but that nonetheless carries the entire weight of the building."

Two years passed after these first revelations. In 1895, because of her husband's job, Conchita and the whole family moved from San Luis Potosí to Mexico City. "On September 28, we went to live in Mexico City," said Conchita in her autobiography.

After these dates, we frequently find the following question and supplication in her *Account of Conscience*: "Lord, how long before the Oasis comes to be?"

On April 4,1896, she wrote: "I petitioned the Lord often for the Oasis, that is, for its founding. And my soul felt that the following year, God would be glorified in this blessed place of privacy. Oh, how I wish it would be so!"

In the meantime, God continued to shower extraordinary graces upon Conchita's soul, preparing her to receive the "transforming union" or "spiritual marriage" which, according to the great mystics, is the highest pinnacle to which God takes his elect during their mortal life. Conchita received this grace on February 9, 1897. The following day she wrote to her spiritual director:

"Last night I was really driven to prayer in a very powerful manner, starting at 1:00 a.m. From the time the Lord woke me up, I felt my soul very filled with his presence, not in the usual way, but in a very special and full manner. I felt, without knowing why, the weight of the Divine Majesty. I was surprised that, upon awakening, I was repeating these words over and over, as though they were naturally overflowing from my heart: 'Most Holy Trinity have mercy on us. You who are one God!' And I could not interrupt these praises.

"And Jesus told me: 'Get up. Here are the Father and the Holy Spirit. They have come because I want to present your soul to them as my betrothed.'

"Oh Father, what mortification this caused me! If the handsomest prince on earth, desired the most horrible of monstrosities, that would not compare with the predicament in which I found myself. It seemed to me absurd, madness, a mistake, something impossible that this would be Jesus' desire. What longing I felt to be good and perfect!

"All I could do was throw myself on the floor and with my face stuck to the ground, experience great humility and confusion. Oh, and why not, feeling the real presence of the three Divine Persons!

"For two hours this burning in my soul would not diminish, until I felt faint, as a result of the extremely intense sentiments of my soul."

Conchita could not explain with words what she had experienced during those two hours. But she told us about one of the effects of that grace:

"A great fire remained burning in my soul. And there also remained an effect which I am still experiencing: a constant increase of love, respect and intimate knowledge (at least one that's not too obscure) of the Holy Trinity. Oh my God, my God! Three in One! Blessed, blessed are you, forever and ever!"

Finally, at the beginning of 1897, Conchita and Father Mir decided that the time had arrived to begin searching for the first vocations for the founding of the Sisters of the Cross. Father Mir invited the associates of the Apostleship of the Cross who stood out in their commitment to the Lord and showed signs of a vocation to the religious life. He found three young women willing to establish the first convent. They rented a house and furnished it with the help of Don Octaviano Cabrera, Conchita's oldest brother. And there, on May 3, 1897 on Calle Real de Popotla, number 24, the first "Oasis" was founded amidst much poverty and simplicity. Conchita was present at the Mass and the blessing of the house. That day she wrote in her diary:

"Thank you, my God, thank you a thousand times! My heart and my lips do not know how to say anything else.

"I have just come back from the blessing of the Oasis. Trembling with emotion, today I stepped on the threshold of that holy house. Lost among the people, I walked through that holy enclosure so sacred to me. After the talks, I had the blessing of having breakfast in the kitchen. Oh, if only I could have stayed there permanently, serving the spouses of Our Lord!"

By the 16th of July, there were already seven postulants. That day, Bishop Ibarra invested them in the habit of the novices. Father Mir gave them daily instruction in the religious life and with much fervor they started to live their new life.

The historical development of the congregation, with its struggles and triumphs, is not within the scope of this book. In this volume, we wish to deal solely with the profundity of the spirit of this congregation as a clear and concrete expression of the school of spirituality that we are studying.

From the present *Constitutions* of the Sisters of the Cross, we have selected those phrases that best illustrate our objective:

God has called the Sisters of the Cross to more closely follow Jesus Christ, Priest and Victim; therefore, guided by the Holy Spirit, they are to resemble Christ and be a permanent offering to the Divine Father for the sake of the Church.

They shall seek God in a life of contemplation, solitude and silence, in voluntary and loving sacrifice, doing humble and simple work. In order to participate in the redemptive offering of Jesus Christ, they shall be united to him in the sacrifice of the Mass and they shall adore him constantly in the Holy Eucharist.

The religious women of this institution shall dispose themselves to continue, in their own lives, the participation of Mary in the offering and the sacrifice of Jesus. She was the hidden victim who would offer herself to the Eternal Father along with Jesus, for the same purpose. She faithfully maintained her union with Jesus unto the Cross. There, her only begotten Son suffered and she united herself to his sacrifice, consenting with love in the immolation of the Victim that she herself engendered.

The Sisters of the Cross have it as a holy duty to supplicate to God that priests be his glory, configured each time more perfectly with the Supreme and Eternal Priest, and that through them, the world of today will receive the grace of God. The motto of this institution and the program of its life are the words of Christ, 'For them I am consecrated.'

The Sisters of the Cross shall unite themselves each day to the Lord's Sacrifice that is renewed in the Eucharist, conscious that this daily participation is the supreme moment in which to offer Christ to the Father and offer themselves in union with him. In this way, they shall progress day by day in the communion of charity with Christ and with the Church, so that God can be all things to all people.

Through the sacrament of Communion, the Sisters of the Cross shall nurture and renew the ardent desire to share in the Passion of Jesus and collaborate with him in the salvation of the world, lovingly taking up the cross each day.

The Holy Sacrament shall be exposed day and night in all the houses of this institution and the life of the community shall revolve around him. Faith in our Lord, present in this mystery, is our path to sanctification and the manner chosen to deepen and continue the offering of the Mass, and to achieve graces for all God's people, especially for priests.

THIRD PERIOD

1898 - 1904

In this chapter we are going to follow, very succinctly, Conchita's spiritual trajectory, from the early part of 1898 until the last part of 1904. These were the years in which our Lord was preparing her for the central grace of her life: the mystical incarnation.

From February 14, 1897, the Lord had announced to Conchita: "Prepare yourself for the day on which the Church celebrates the Incarnation of the Word. On that day, I descended to unite myself to Mary, taking flesh in her most pure womb, to save the world. On that day I want to unite myself spiritually to your soul and give you a new life, for now and for eternity. Prepare yourself, purify yourself, because the grace for which you are preparing is very great."

Conchita understood that she would receive the promised grace on March 25 of that year, but the Lord prepared her for nine long years, perfecting his servant through many and varied mystical experiences, as well as through much pain and suffering, both physical and spiritual.

Conchita's humility was forever growing. Here is an example: "I spent an hour before the Most Blessed Sacrament, and during that prayer, I saw my corruption and my loathsomeness rising before the eyes of God. At the height of my shame, I said to Jesus: 'Tell me, Jesus, frankly, do you not find me truly disgusting and repugnant? How can it not be so, since I see myself that way?' And Jesus answered me: 'Precisely because you see yourself as such, you do not disgust me.'"

As far as her progress in prayer, let's read some examples of the enlightenment that Conchita received during this period:

"After receiving Communion, I felt a divine impulse and I allowed myself to be carried away by the will of God. I scarcely did this and my soul was suspended at a fixed point, and that point was God. I saw or felt something that had never occurred to me: the eternal generation that is of God. That is, how from all eternity the Father begets the Word, remaining two distinct Persons, but with a single substance, with one will and one power. And in that same moment, a pleasure, a love, a union arises between the two Divine Persons that produce the third Divine Person, the Holy Spirit. He is indispensable between the Father and the Son, so that without him, they could not be. This unity forms the joy of heaven. And to think that this God in three distinct Persons, but with one eternal love, is the One contained within the smallest part of a consecrated host!"

During this time, the communications with Jesus not only became more frequent, but the Holy Spirit also communicated with her many times. Conchita spoke with great frequency of the "touches" and of the "repose" that she received from the Divine Spirit, and also of her familiar conversations with him.

For example: "Being in prayer, I felt the presence of the Holy Spirit; thinking about the songs of the doves that I saw on the haciendas, I asked if he used to sing.

"'Yes,' he answered me promptly, 'but my song can be heard only in heaven, because a human creature would die upon hearing it. You see, little daughter, there is much ice in souls because they do not call upon me. They do not ascend the Cross, and because of that, they do not come to me. In only a few souls am I able to make my nest; only in those that are empty of themselves, in those that do not have their eyes fixed on earthly things. I fill those souls with my presence. Blessed is the spirit that is consecrated to me. I will make it holy. I will give it my gifts and it will know an inner life full of enlightenment and I will reveal to it the mysteries hidden from the greater part of humankind. I am the light that illumines and the fire that heats. I am he who gives grace, who instills virtues and who purifies hearts. I am Life and my Being is the communication of love.'"

Time went on, and God continued his marvelous work in Conchita's soul. On the outside, she did everything she could to fulfill her family duties with perfection. In February 1898, her eighth child was born, a girl whom she named Guadalupe; during the following year, also in February, her ninth child, Pedro, was born.

During this last pregnancy, Conchita suffered from phlebitis in both legs; after the birth, she became ill with appendicitis. She was so ill that everyone thought she would die, but she survived the illness. Conchita wrote: "I was on the brink of death. I am able to say that I touched the tomb. I told Jesus: 'Let's go, Lord; let's go, if you wish; only pardon me for how much I have offended you.'"

Finally, she returned to health, although never completely. Her love of God, for each of the three Divine Persons, always continued to grow: "I saw the three most blessed Persons, I don't know how, in an admirable union, without ever being able to separate One from the Other, but the three participate in everything, always eternally. Their communication is admirable and constant. A communication of light in the same Light, of divinity in the same Divinity, of joy in the same Joy, of perfection and eternal and indefinable love. It is there; there is the center of life; it is Life itself.

"I see a special joy among the three Divine Persons upon contemplating themselves, reflecting their beauty and their perfection, One to the Other; this always without tiring, ecstatic in their infinite and eternal delight. I see how they take pleasure in the intimacy of their mystery, to where not even the angels can go, to where nobody has penetrated, nor will penetrate.

"I see how this Holy Trinity is creating without diminishing itself, giving of itself without lessening, overflowing torrentially; because the Trinity is the fount of grace and of life. The Trinity is the essence of all that exists and all that will exist; it is outside the boundaries of time, a boundless immensity, a sea without shores in each of its attributes.

"This contemplation brings me a detachment from the world and from myself, and a desire to be there above – and when will it be? – immersed in the complete possession of that which I now barely discern."

Nine days later, she wrote in her diary: "My soul is elevated in prayer, united with God even among people, and with a desire for solitude. Every once in a while, the Lord collects me, in that loving silence. I feel the divine contact of an Infinite, Holy, and Pure Being: of my God the Holy Spirit. I wish for nothing more than to be in deep prayer, contemplating him. Oh, my God! Who am I, a poor animal, that you would communicate with me like this? If you were not God, I would tell you that you do not know what you are doing; you throw your perfume into a vessel of filthy clay and toss your pearls into a pigsty. Lord, Lord! I am mud and nothing more!"

Sometimes, the Lord gave her these lessons: "I was before the Most Blessed Sacrament for one hour; but the more I did to collect myself, nothing happened; I remained with a bunch of imaginings in my head, and almost unbelievable distractions. Finally, upon leaving, I heard the voice of the Lord that said to me: 'Now do you see? Have you convinced yourself that when I do not give to you, you have nothing?'"

With the following phrases, during 1899 and 1900, Conchita intends to summarize her spiritual life: "What a heterogeneous life! Days when my soul is ardent, and then days with a frozen soul. Days of constant prayer and, suddenly, dry as a bone."

In October of 1899, we find a paragraph in which Conchita wanted to explain a new style of prayer that she called "prayer of love":

"The soul, understanding its insignificance, and wanting to have more to give to the Beloved, asks to love him with his own love, because that which the soul can give him is poor and lukewarm; then the creature remains annihilated, without a will of its own, totally surrendered to the divine will; this is a very elevated prayer, in which the nothing is united to the All. Oh, if I could better explain how this transformation occurs in the most intimate areas of the heart!"

Theology tells us that we will know God in heaven, not with the enlightenment of our intelligence, but with the participation of the divine intelligence; that we will love God, not with our poor human love, but with the participation of the love with which God loves himself and loves us. However, God concedes some first fruits from this life to the mystics, a little preview of heaven, a tiny taste of that eternal banquet, in which we will all participate.

In March of 1900, Conchita had a new experience of prayer which she tried to explain as follows:

"The Lord gave me a type of very exalted prayer, of which I had no idea, and it was the first time that I had experienced it. It was a direct encounter of the soul with God. I believe that in this way, God will ask the soul for an accounting when one dies. There are no encumbrances in this prayer, nor does one go through stages. It is not the soul that looks for God, but rather it is God that attracts the soul to his presence. What a marvelous thing! He elevated my spirit directly toward him! In an instant, the Divine Majesty pulled the poor worm, and I saw my soul totally exposed before my God. I was not afraid – how strange! – except that I experienced a profound humility and complete trust. I saw myself as poor as I am and I saw him so full of all that is good, and it made me ask him for humility, purity and holiness.

"I will explain it better with an example. If a person were to tell another that he was in the king's good favor, that person would believe it, but not with absolute certainty. But there is a different type of certainty when we see the King without mediators and he affirms us of his friendship directly. That is how this prayer was: a direct interview with the Lord that left me with a type of security regarding his purest friendship.

"This type of prayer brings with it a healthy confusion and at the same time a great trust in God, because in an instant it elevates the soul and throws it into the arms of the most wonderful Father, its Lord and God. 'Yes, Lord, yes!,' the embarrassed soul then says to him before such beauty, 'it is certain that I have offended you and that I am horrible, but oh, Lord!, you also see that I love you; that I adore you with all of my strength; that I want to serve you and to be yours, to live and to die in hidden sacrifice; and only for you, my God, because I love you with my whole being, because you are my love, my joy, my only desire and happiness, on earth and in heaven. If I had a thousand lives and a thousand hearts, I would consecrate them all to you without even one beat of my heart that would not be for you. My spirit and all my being flies toward you as its center. You are my Everything. I was born for you, my God. You are my destiny; I desire only to possess you and to have your love. What do you want me to do? In what way do you wish to employ this heart that you have pierced? Speak, Lord, your servant is listening. Receive all that I am and all that I have; you have given everything to me; it is yours and I return it to you.'

"In this prayer, with the same ray of light that God grants to the soul, he makes the soul to know him and to know itself, to receive him and to give itself, to love and to see itself loved. What greatness and kindness of the Lord, beyond words, toward a poor and miserable creature!

"This step is so high for the soul, and its effects so very pure, that there is no way the creature can achieve it, nor should it even dare to wish for it; for it depends totally on the Lord; and only he, taking the soul when he wishes, can introduce it into such intimate and hidden regions."

During these years, Conchita wrote in her diary various times what the Lord taught her about the suffering received through love. The following are some randomly selected paragraphs:

"A thirst for suffering has grown in me, because I clearly see the hidden treasure which this contains. We should run toward that holy suffering which purifies and sanctifies, and which ignites the divine fire in the soul. The Lord makes me see that suffering is the center of the most pure and unselfish love, and suffering is what unites us most to God, making us like Jesus Christ, the King of Suffering.

"I see – I don't know how – the Lord's plan, demanding of the soul the first step of self-denial, which is mastering its natural repugnance for embracing suffering; if the soul takes this first step with generosity and courage and only because it loves the Lord, he will make the soul happy and will cause the curtain to be raised that covered the treasure hidden by the bark of the Cross, and reveal to the eyes of the soul in love the infinite delights of suffering for love.

"I see all of this by a stroke of divine enlightenment and I feel it and experience it; but I also understand that not everyone sees it the same way, and I am sorrowful to feel such a great error. I see clearly how the Lord came to show us the richness of suffering by his life and by his example, out of pure love; it pains my soul to see how the world rejects suffering or fears it, and the many evils that come from that.

"I am aware that suffering torments the soul and the body. I feel its negative qualities, and I see its frightening aspects that terrify nature. But I also see as clearly as the light of day that all of this that horrifies is only the outer shell, and that behind this veil one may encounter heaven.

"Besides, and this is very important, the Lord is always there, like the most generous Cyrenian, to assist us in carrying the cross; and he will never place on our shoulders a cross that is heavier than we can bear.

"I see the Lord as a skilled swimmer who is hidden, but who loves much and has such a compassionate heart that it is pure love. Well then, as the soul hurls itself with all of its good will and longing toward the immense sea of the cross, he hurls himself in its wake and although he allows it to feel the shock of the waters and even the anguish of death, he never lets it sink or drown, but measures with his infinite wisdom exactly what is necessary for its purification.

"And afterwards, how the soul believes, hopes, and loves with an increased purity and with admirable bursts of the most pristine love that it has ever known!"

During Conchita's life, the "nights of the soul" and attacks of the enemy were also abundant. Only God knows why it is necessary for his chosen to pass through such trials. On July 14th, 1901, she wrote in her *Account of Conscience:*

"Since yesterday, a terrible storm has been unleashed within my soul, with very intense struggles. Oh my God! I am spent, without strength from so many tears and so much suffering. I cannot endure anymore. I scare myself: it is as if being condemned is of little importance to me; as if with just a bit more diabolic influence I would offend God in some way. My God! What is happening to me? I find myself so often loving God and at the same time wanting to run away from this internal prompting. I am ashamed to appear before him, and I do not want to glance into my soul. My head is overwhelmed, my heart frozen, my reason darkened, my imagination unleashed and without restraint. Jesus, Jesus, have compassion for me!"

From that day until September 8th (almost two months), Conchita wrote in her diary of a "deep sadness," of "extreme dryness," of "temptations against the faith," of "glacial indifference." But it always ended with expressions such as this: "It is an accumulation of suffering that I have often tried to explain but which has always remained without explanation. But on with the Cross and blessed be the Lord!"

On the twelfth day of the same month of September, she wrote: "My husband, very sick. A very bad night. My soul suffers great pain in seeing him suffer. Blessed be the Lord for everything!"

Here her diary breaks off and it does not resume until September 27th. It begins with these words:

"I am a widow. How much pain! How much suffering! I saw how my husband's life was slipping away moment by moment, and as I saw his parting grow nearer, the affection of my heart was magnified. He became gravely ill. Death came – my God! – and he regained consciousness! Several times I prayed the prayers of the dying for him. My four oldest children surrounded his bed until his death. I would just repeat: 'Your will be done on earth as it is in heaven.' And I felt the strength of the Holy Spirit that enabled me to peacefully accept the terrible blow.

"At seven in the evening the Lord took my husband, after having given him to me on earth for 16 years and 10 months. The Lord gave him to me, the Lord took him from me. Blessed be his Holy Name!"

Conchita began her "new life," alone with her eight children, six boys and two girls. The oldest was sixteen and the youngest was two years and seven months of age. She was going to be thirty-nine years old.

A few months later she wrote: "The wound has not healed as yet. I cannot erase from my mind the memory of my husband who was the only love of my life. I didn't even imagine how much I loved him until I lost him. I am not able to pray, because as soon as I collect myself, the memories of my husband come to my mind and the tears flow without consolation... Oh, my God! It seems to me that I am lacking greater faith, but I want to live by it!

"Before now I had not realized just how much I loved my husband. I loved him as a spouse, as a father and as a brother and on

45

losing him, my heart has been torn by pain and this wound continues to bleed.

"Oh Lord, be a thousand times blessed! I kiss your holy hand and I adore and respect your inscrutable plans. Why do you leave me alone during the most bitter days of my life?"

Later, the cross of infirmities arrived. In August of 1902, Conchita became ill with typhoid, was given up as having no hope of recovery by the doctors and received the last rites. A month later, her six year old son, Salvador, contracted diphtheria and was in danger of death. Shortly after, Pablito suffered a fall that had serious consequences. And as a consequence of so many sleepless nights and excessive exertion, a cerebral anemia settled upon her. In these circumstances, she wrote:

"Today I feel very ill. I can hardly lift the pen. Blessed be God and may he make me and all that belongs to me pleasing to him! I am his and therefore I do not belong to myself. May his divine and most holy will be done, now and forever!"

Months later, she wrote: "How profound is the mystery of suffering! But it comes to be discovered by the soul that surrenders itself to the divine will in loving sacrifice, abandoning itself for pure love. For me, suffering has been a grace. I experience, almost palpably, how it purifies me and cleanses me, how it lightens my spirit from the dregs of the earth and from its own wants, how it has lifted my spirit to the heights that, without suffering, it would never have known. What richness and sublimity comes from the Cross! But many do not understand it because they have denied themselves the experience.

"At times I have very vivid insights regarding the value of suffering when it is accepted because of love. And I ask God to draw back the mysterious veil that covers this treasure for other souls. Because the human heart is always fleeing from its happiness, and believing it has found it, it hurls itself toward what it is not and abandons the only thing that can give it: the Cross, embraced with love.

"Only in the depth of voluntary affliction is the soul transformed completely in charity. It is in this sacrificial suffering where it certainly dies in order to be born anew, no longer thinking of itself, because there, all selfishness is extinguished. There it lives purely and willingly for God and for others and reaches celestial peace."

In her writings during 1902, Conchita accentuated her interest in the salvation of all souls. In these lines, for example: "My soul burns with the desire to attain the salvation and perfection of many. I would like to be a preacher and sing and shout the riches of the Cross to the four winds. The Lord allowed me to know – I don't know how – that I should give myself to others; that I should use the rest of my life for the good of others; that I should consume myself for the good of souls, employing all of my strength and faculties in bringing them to God.

"It seems to me that charity, or love of others, has taken up a greater part of my heart. I want to give my life and my blood and spend myself in favor of the salvation of everyone. I have a thirst for seeing light shine in souls, allowing them to know the Divine Heart, pierced and suffering out of pure love."

On February 4th, 1903, Conchita met Father Felix of Jesus Rougier, a French priest from the Congregation of Mary. The Lord revealed to Conchita that he had chosen Father Felix to found the congregation of the "Religious of the Cross," of which he had spoken since 1897. We will speak of this founding in due time.

On April 7th of that year (1903), the tragic death of the youngest of her children, Pedrito, who was only four years of age, was added to Conchita's internal suffering.

It was Holy Tuesday; Conchita was sewing in her room and her children were playing in the garden. Suddenly, she heard a voice

47

that said to her: "Pedrito is in the fountain," and she was terrified. She left the house shouting: "Pedrito is in the fountain!" And all of the children ran toward it. When Conchita arrived, they told her: "Yes, Mamá, he is there." And there was Pedrito, drowned in the very shallow fountain. Conchita narrated that "she felt like a crazy woman, and tried everything possible to try to bring him back to life." When the doctor arrived, he discovered a mark from the water faucet key on the child's forehead. The child had slipped, striking himself on the faucet key, had lost consciousness and had drowned in a few centimeters of water.

Conchita held vigil over the body of her little son throughout the night. On the following day, Holy Wednesday, she attended the burial. All of her children accompanied her, as well as Father Felix, who went with them to the cemetery of Tepeyac, to bless the grave. Later, Conchita said, "Father Felix spoke to my soul, supporting my faith and my sacrifice. And I, uniting my suffering to that of the Sacred Heart, offered my son for the salvation of souls, for the sanctification of priests and for the Works of the Cross."

Father Felix, a true saint, was Conchita's second spiritual director and although his direction lasted only a year, it produced excellent fruit for that chosen soul.

On July 15, 1904, Father Felix, convinced that God was calling him to found the "Religious of the Cross," left for France to speak personally with Father Antonio Martín, superior general of his congregation and to obtain permission for the new order.

We know well what happened through a letter that Father Martín wrote in response to one which Conchita had written:

> If I were sure that this is God's will, I would not hesitate for even a moment in giving Father Felix the permission that he requests. But I have no more proof of this other than your affirmation, which does not suffice, as sincere

as it may be. Regarding revelations or private visions, illusions are likely, even in very good and holy people. Proof is lacking that you have not fooled yourself into believing that this is God's will. Moreover, until the authority of the Church grants its judgment, it would be extremely dangerous to make a decision supported only by what you say.

I have put everything before the members of my Council, who are pious religious, instructed and experienced in the spiritual direction of souls; and following their recommendation, I have reached the decision of which you are aware. If we have made a mistake, God will inform us of our error and in that case, there will be no opposition on my part, but on the contrary, my complete support in the fulfillment of God's plans for Father.

In reality, Father Martín proceeded with the proper prudence. He sent Father Felix to teach at an elementary school that the Marists had in Barcelona and prohibited him from communicating with Mrs. Armida. Father Felix faithfully obeyed the orders of his superior and with admirable faith in God waited ten years for the requested permission.

FOURTH PERIOD

1905 - 1906

It is now time to study the principal or central grace in Conchita's life which, as we have said, was the mystical incarnation. She received this grace on March 25th, 1906. The months that preceded this were a period of intense preparation. These were months of much suffering, both of body and soul; months of profound purification by means of the humble and loving acceptance of pain.

In January of 1905, a sore formed on Conchita's foot. Considering its persistence and malignance, the doctor concluded that it might be cancerous. A brother of Conchita, named José, had died of cancer after much suffering, so Conchita was filled with anguish:

"I trembled with the prospect of pain and death, but most of all, over the thought of leaving my seven children, who would be orphaned if the Lord were to call me. My soul has received a terrible shock. I want what Jesus wants, but it is difficult to suppress my maternal love. Blessed be God in everything!

"I am yours, Lord. My body and my soul, fortunately, belong to you. If it be your will that they gradually remove parts of my body, then it is my will also. If you want me to die, then I want that, too."

In addition to the pain of the illness, Conchita encountered other suffering: on February 20th, her mother died; in March her godchild José Luis, son of her sister Emilia, also died and in October, her sister Clara passed away.

On top of all this, one must add the internal trials of the "dark night of the soul;" and all of this had repercussions on her character; she felt very humbled by all that was happening.

"I want to explode at every setback, and they are not few. It causes me much pain to have this nature of a lion or snake; everything causes me to lose my patience, and the more I try, the more useless it is.

"And Jesus remains hidden, always silent. He doesn't want to talk to me. I suffer much and I am dying without him. I feel so alone, with such an emptiness in my soul. I need Jesus. I spend hours at his feet, but often I feel like a block of ice, or I just remain there amidst many tears. Blessed be God, but I cannot carry on. Mary, mother of my soul, have compassion for me!"

A few days later, she wrote this prayer: "Oh my God, my God! My heart is anxious to possess you and to love you without ceasing, burning constantly with a hunger for you. And where are you, Lord of my life? Where have you gone, Life of my soul, that I cannot find you? Oh, without a doubt, my failure to respond to you has distanced you from me. What can I do, my Love, to find you again? My soul is restless, desolate and disturbed, because it cannot find rest in you. Oh my Jesus Christ, don't leave me; don't hide from me – have mercy. What can I do without you? You know I can do nothing without the help of your grace. Don't you love me anymore? I shall always love you. This life will surely end anyway, and then... Oh, Life of my life, my Love and my All! Then I shall find you and listen to you throughout eternity."

Under these circumstances, her spiritual director, Archbishop Maximino Ruiz, gave her an admirable piece of advice: "Remain in poverty even from the things of God."

This advice was in conformity with that of all teachers of the spiritual life. They urge a complete detachment, not just from all worldly things, but also from the consolations or palpable experiences that God grants at the beginning of the journey and that he later removes so that the soul no longer seeks the consolations of God but rather God himself, accepting a life guided only by faith and hope. Conchita commented in the following way regarding this advice:

"Oh my God, my director tells me to enter into poverty even from you; that is, that I unite my will to yours, accepting that you are hiding from me, even if it means not hearing from you until eternity. I am working now on this detachment even from your gifts, but this causes my soul to bleed. It feels like I am tearing out my own heart. Now I shall truly remain poor, but rich in the Cross. But is it not true, Love of my loves, that in this richness I shall have my Jesus? Oh, yes, I shall possess him very closely and hold him tightly against my poor heart!"

Conchita called this situation the "sorrowful union" because she felt united to Jesus, but to the crucified Jesus who shouted, "My God, my God, why have you abandoned me?" (Mt 27:46)

"Nail me onto the backside of your Cross, if you want. And if you desire it, give me the grace of your helplessness, your abandonment, your desolation. I shall love you just the same. Oh Jesus, my Jesus! Is it not true that we have both tasted from the same sweetness and now we drink from the same chalice?"

A few days later, she wrote this prayer: "Oh my Jesus, in the midst of my coldness, I love you. Hidden in your apparent disdain, I love you. In my doubts, in my struggles, in my pain, I love you. Amidst my deceased ones and the memories that pierce my heart, I love you. In a future so obscure, in my poverty and in my solitude, I love you. In the midst of the scorn of many and the bewilderment of those whom I love the most, I love you; from the corner in which you have placed me, I love you, Jesus, I love you!..."

By means of these expressions, we discover how Conchita's love had been purified through the path of suffering, until it had become a total and selfless abandonment, firm and irrevocable. It was this state of submission and absolute obedience to the divine will that Conchita referred to as being a VICTIM in union with Jesus, for the love of the Father and the salvation of many souls. This is the essence of the Spirituality of the Cross.

Thus we come to January of 1906. Conchita had a few brief visions of Jesus wherein she always saw him in his passion, or dying on the Cross. On January 6th, she wrote:

53

"Very close to Jesus in the Blessed Sacrament, I let go a flood of tears and I renewed my offering as victim for whatever might be pleasing to God. Then I felt this powerful attraction, like a magnet that drags the soul and attaches it to its God. I am certain that this is a true union. But it is a painful union, a powerful similitude that, amidst tears, binds my will closely to that of Christ, causing my soul to desire more and more to be a victim in a holocaust pleasing to the Lord. It seems to me that this union in pain is the closest connection in which a soul can exist with Jesus, because within it reigns a total love that unites the two wills onto the same Cross."

At this time, Conchita experienced growth in her spiritual life. She realized that God was preparing her for something, although she did not understand what it was.

"It seems to me that my spirit has passed through another door in the spiritual life. I truly feel I am entering another phase, as if ascending a new stairway; and what I ask of God is that all be fulfilled according to his divine will."

Later, she was enlightened concerning a very important truth: All that we have has no value before God, but only to the extent that we are united to his Son. It is necessary to live with him, for him and in him. Only thus will the Father accept our offerings of self, our works, or our sufferings.

"Every day I see more clearly that I can do nothing for God, and even though I truly have advanced in my prayer, in my detachment from all earthly creatures, in my poverty and in other areas, I feel my hands are empty…

"The Lord has enlightened me to understand the reason for these contradictory sentiments – of progress and emptiness at the same time. The more clearly I see God, the more I perceive the great distance which separates us – what he deserves and the little I am and the little I can offer to him. I see the truth with all clarity, the smallness of my being, the lowliness of my acts, my imperfections, my nothingness….

"Oh my Jesus! It doesn't surprise me any more to feel this emptiness, this immense void in my works. I only desire that these works reflect you, you who are of such great worth.

"I need him to be in everything that I am, as I myself disappear. That way, I will not suffer in finding everything empty, depleted and without value. I will not suffer in not having anything of worth to give to God. I will gather all in my Jesus. I will no longer be me, but Jesus in me: he in my thoughts, in my soul, in my actions, and sacrifices, and work, and rest, and at night, and during the day, and while asleep, and while awake, and at all times, always, always, always…"

In February, she received new enlightenment from the Lord regarding the distinction between the gifts she had received from God and what was of herself. She recognized, and was grateful for so many undeserved favors, but she felt no vanity, because they were riches from God and not of herself:

"I would like to put the eyeglasses of truth on people, so they could see how I truly am. I am like a donkey, dark and full of worms, that is carrying a treasure of gold. I am like a poisonous snake covered with sparkling diamonds. I am a cadaver inside a coffin of pure silver. I would like to hide in the sewer, out of pure shame to face my God, and face the people who think I am so good.

"How is it, Life of my soul, that I dare to approach you? It is because the more I discover my impoverishment, the more I feel the need to come to your grandeur; it is that my nothing needs your Everything."

On March 20th, Conchita started her spiritual exercises with the Sisters of the Cross. On the 23rd, two days before receiving that aforementioned enormous grace, Conchita wrote in her diary:

"Coming from my room, I entered the chapel to pay a short visit to Jesus. Upon kneeling, I heard his voice, which told me:

"'I want you to be mine.'

"'Am I not yours already, Jesus, my Adored One?'

"'I want you to belong to me completely, that all your affections be for me. I want that place in your heart where I can rest, cleansed from all dust.'

"I was embarrassed and at the same time anxious to purify myself, to truly wash this vile heart for him, this heart that nevertheless belonged solely to him. I am going to confession, as these words have moved me to contrition."

The next day she wrote: "The meditation regarding the Incarnation of the Word made me shudder, because I have had an unresolved matter with him for some time now. I am ashamed and do not even want to look him in the face, because without a doubt, I have not been in compliance with his plans. Maybe I seem so horrible to him that he has changed his mind, for his honor.

"Oh forgive me, Lord, and have mercy on me! This incarnate Word enamors me, rouses me and captivates me. The work of the Holy Spirit within the womb of Mary! In her, he poured out his omnipotence and his love. The Incarnation of the Word has for me the most pleasing aromas, the flavor of the Eucharist, celestial enchantments, incomprehensible sweetness, ineffable delights, unknown riches that only God can grant. And why should I receive such a favor? I perceive your touch, Holy Trinity, and my stunned soul is filled with gratitude and love.

"When I read that he came unto his own but his own received him not, I suffer to consider that, although I am so much his, I, too, have not yet received him because I am so unworthy of such a favor. But nevertheless I love him. Oh, yes, I love him more than my life, more than a thousand lives and a thousand heavens. My poor heart feels an unimaginable tenderness for this Word, for this Eternal Word of God.

"And tomorrow is his feast and I have nothing to offer him and I feel like dying of shame and embarrassment. All I have is this crude, cold and dreadful cross... Do you recognize it, my Divine Word? Do you accept it? Let me cry and tell you a thousand times that I love you. This is what I am!"

These were the sentiments of the Servant of God when March 25th arrived, the Feast of the Annunciation of the Lord.

On that day, she received a most special favor and Conchita tried to describe it in her *Account of Conscience*. She spoke thus:

"Day 25th. The Feast of the Annunciation of the Lord. 5th day of the exercises.

"Trembling with embarrassment, stunned, and beaten to the ground, oh my God, oh my God! I come today with my soul overflowing, like a fountain that brims over because it doesn't have the space to contain the abundant overflow. This is how I come today, overflowing and embarrassed, to empty myself out on paper.

"In the first 'memento' of the Mass, I felt the presence of Jesus beside me and I listened to his voice, which told me:

'Here I am. I want to incarnate mystically in your heart. I fulfill what I promise. I have been preparing you for this in a thousand ways, and the moment has arrived to fulfill my promise. RECEIVE ME.'

"I felt joy and an inexpressible embarrassment. I thought Jesus was talking about Communion. But he, reading my thoughts, continued:

"'Today you have received me in a different manner. I have taken possession of your heart. I incarnate myself mystically there so as to never be separated from you. This is a great grace that my goodness has prepared in you. Be humble and grateful.'

"'But Lord', I dared to say to him, 'what was it that you offered me, that you asked of me? Was it not a betrothal?'

"'That has already passed. This grace is infinitely greater.'

"'Is this a spiritual matrimony, my Jesus?'

"'It is even more, because matrimony is more of an external union: But this is to incarnate, to live and to grow in your soul, without ever leaving it. This is my possessing you and you possessing me as if forming one single substance – not so much you giving me your life, as I giving my life to your soul. This is a compenetration that you cannot understand. This is the grace of all graces.'

"And understanding without wanting to understand, I told him:

"'Are you a child within my soul, my Jesus?'

"'I can incarnate not only as a child, but in any manner in which I please. This is, I repeat, a grand and elevated mystical union, the greatest there can be. It is just like in heaven except that in heaven the Divine veil is lifted...'

"'But I am not worthy of this, my Jesus!'

"'Nobody is worthy. Love me, imitate me, and never allow yourself to be separated from me. This type of union is very deep, very intimate, and if you are faithful, it is eternal. And I will give you new life. Breathe it in. It is holy, it is the life of your Jesus; it is he himself, who is life.'

"'I am the Word, who has loved you for all eternity and I have prepared you for this day. Carry me always with this very real and effective presence in your soul.'

"I truly felt a union with him, something that was alive and palpitating in my soul. And my spirit was filled with freshness, peace, and an infinite delight. Oh, how can I reciprocate? Lord, Lord! What else can I do but humble myself and ask Mary to give you thanks on my behalf and imitate her, saying in my lowliness, 'Here is the servant of the Lord, let it be done to me according to your word!'"

We already know that in religious language, words frequently express only an analogy or similarity. For example, the words

"Father," "Son," "Holy Spirit," "spiritual matrimony"... are words that attempt to give us an idea of realities not readily expressible in our everyday language. This is because our process of understanding has to flow from the known to the unknown, from the material to the spiritual.

That is why the expression "mystical incarnation" is solely an analogy, a similitude, but, of course, it expresses a REALITY.

This reality is an extraordinary union and an exceptional presence of the Word within a soul predestined for this grace. That is why the Lord told Conchita that through this favor she had been converted into a "living tabernacle" or a "consecrated host." These also are comparisons that explain the same thing: presence and union. But we need to take into consideration that analogies in the mystical language are expressions that signify a reality far greater than that with which they are compared.

Finally, let us consider two texts in the Gospel: "The one who loves me listens to my words and my Father will love him. And my Father and I will come and dwell with him permanently" (Jn 14:23).

"Looking at those who were seated around him, he said, 'These are my mother, my brothers and my sisters. Whoever does the will of God is my brother, my sister, and my mother" (Mk 3:34).

The first text teaches us that the reward for one who obeys the word of Jesus is a predilection from the Father, by which the believer will enjoy a special presence of the same Father and of Jesus.

In the second, Christ magnificently expresses his love for the person who loves everyone on earth, which does not exclude loving one's mother.

But why speak in this book of the mystical incarnation? What does this very personal grace of Conchita have to do with the Spirituality of the Cross, which is for everyone? I will explain.

It is certain that we are not all called to these extraordinary graces. We should not desire them or ask for them, precisely because they are "extraordinary," apart from the normal in the life of faith. God gives them to whomever he pleases and a person can do nothing to deserve them.

Nevertheless, all of us who want to live the spirituality of Christ, Priest and Victim, are called to live in a growing union with the Word Incarnate. He is our constant offering to the Father and, with him, we offer ourselves for the same goals as his Incarnation and his death on the Cross. Thus the grace of the mystical incarnation granted to Conchita is like a goal, unreachable but illuminating, just as the moon which we cannot touch guides our steps through the night.

In addition, it teaches us many practical things. For example, it shows us the value of sacramental Communion. I think that this is an enormous grace and the closest in similarity to the mystery of the Incarnation in each one of us. Is it not the same holy body that Mary engendered which remains united to us during Communion; and with him, the human soul of Christ and the Divine Word, inseparable from the Father and the Holy Spirit? Oh, when will we have a greater appreciation and when will we be more aware of the momentous significance of each Communion! One single Communion, properly received, is enough to make us holy!

Also upon analyzing what happened in the life of Conchita after this grace, we learn that our life on earth will always be a life of faith; and that even the greatest experiences of God are transitory. They do not take away that obscure quality of our faith, of our waiting, sometimes so very prolonged.

Another lesson is the simplicity and humility of Conchita, even though she received so many special privileges from God. After the mystical incarnation, we see her devoted to her sewing and her humble chores in the kitchen and in the house, imitating the most humble mother of Jesus. This teaches us that although we may receive great gifts from the Lord, they do not change the fact that every individual has to sanctify him or herself by fulfilling the duties of his or her state in life with love and perfection.

Now that the purpose of this chapter has been explained, let us view the effects that the mystical incarnation produced in the soul and in the life of the servant of God from the same perspective.

A few days after the mystical incarnation, Jesus spoke to Conchita. She explained:

"Upon arriving at the chapel of the Oasis, I had just given Jesus the flower that I take to him every day, offering it with all my love. Suddenly he told me:

"'You can no longer be alone, but rather with me. And I bring heaven within me.

"'I am the Life. I do not need life; I Am Life – not a life composed of moments, but an eternal life; not an ephemeral life, but one that is always perfect; not just in parts, but always whole. This life is my essence; the essence of the three Divine Persons, the Divinity.

"'I am the only nourishment that sustains and conserves. My Being is in giving myself and revealing myself. The ultimate goal of any soul is to transform itself into me, and commensurate with this transformation is the eternal reward. Outside of me, all is death, all is error, because I am the Truth.'"

A little later, we find this paragraph: "I am no longer myself, but Jesus in me. That is how I feel in a very powerful way. I feel a new life. It is as though he has taken absolute possession of my soul and everything in me is subordinate to his action. Oh, my God, what wonders! Such a powerful union!"

Three days later, she wrote: "At home or in the street, amidst the crowds, in conversations and daily duties, I do not let go of the vision of my Beloved. I visit him frequently, I talk to him, I caress him and say a thousand tender endearments to him, and nobody knows this except him. It is beautiful that the world is not aware of these holy intimacies between Jesus and me."

May 3rd: "I feel as though I am deeply absorbed in God. What a living presence of my Lord! I walk among people, but my heart feeds on the Divine Being that I carry within my soul."

May 10th: "With a living and real presence, Jesus is today making himself felt in my soul. He draws me in, he absorbs me and he invites me to imitate him, to follow him closely, to be a living reflection of him crucified."

May 14th: "The Lord asks me to empty out my heart, especially of myself. He exhorts me to keep my thoughts solely in him, that my words be of him, through him and for him."

June 7th: "The Lord has taught me a silent contemplation, without words, without even thinking. The soul just loves, loves; it tells everything to its Beloved through that silent language of divine love. What a beautiful prayer! It is as though a great blaze has absorbed a tiny flame.

"For some time now, this kind of prayer, as well as my spiritual journaling, are the only kinds of prayer that I can accomplish."

June 17th: "Jesus is very quiet, but he remains working in my soul. His glance bathes me, encourages me, enriches me, and absorbs me into the Holy Trinity. He reveals to me infinite mysteries regarding the attributes of God and his inexpressible tenderness, conceivable solely in the heart of God. I see the goodness, the power and the wisdom of God come down to his poor creatures and communicate his divine breath to them. I see how the Holy Trinity gives himself in millions of graces for souls."

October 9th: "My nights are now semi-divine. During the many times that I awaken, he, he alone reigns in my thoughts, in my heart, in all my soul."

At the end of this month, Jesus spoke with Conchita: "'I, upon incarnating myself mystically in your heart, bring with me all the virtues, because they are inseparable from me. And how can I not communicate them to you?'

"'But, my Jesus, it has been some time now and I do not feel these virtues....'

"'Why do you want to feel them? Their effects are enough for you. You are blind to many of the things I accomplish in your soul; how many times have I told you so! But it is one thing that you cannot see them and another thing that they do not exist. There is a big difference.'

"'Jesus, my Jesus, I want to be holy. Carrying that very Sweetness in my soul, how can I be sour or bitter with others? Carrying Charity in its essence, how can I criticize anyone? Carrying Humility, how can I be proud? How can I be angry, when I carry Patience; or hard, when I carry Tenderness; or cold, when I am filled with Fire; or insensitive, when I am filled with Love? Oh my Jesus! I will not be bad from now on, nor deaf to your inspirations, nor impatient, nor so horrible."

Through some letters that Conchita wrote at this time to her friend Mrs. Guadalupe Sánchez de Cerdán, we see how Conchita behaved in her daily life as mother and head of household.

"I went to take care of all of Ignacio's school needs with the Marists. And I am sewing clothes for the little ones who have none for the awards ceremony.

"I withdrew Concha from the school run by the Sisters because I see that it is not good for her to be in the company of such vain and haughty young ladies. Besides, she is now sixteen, and it is time she helps me in the house, with the washing, the cooking, and the mending. I think this is best for her."

In her next letter to the same friend, she told her: "The children are out of school and have passed their exams, thank God.

Nacho got honorable mention and Manuel received many medals. Lupita graduated to 9th grade. Pablo and Salvador also passed and now I have three at home on vacation; imagine that!"

Toward the end of 1906, Lupita developed a tumor in her armpit. They had to operate on her twice. On the day of her second operation, Conchita wrote: "Today was a day of pain and tears. Lupita is suffering greatly. The treatments are terrible and I am always by her side. Oh my God, thy will be done on earth as it is in heaven. I would like to be at the feet of the Lord, but my obligations have not permitted it. Blessed be the Lord!"

On November 12th of that year, her fifteen-year-old son, Manuel, decided to enter the novitiate of the Jesuits, which was located on the hacienda "El Llano" in Michoacán. He was the son who was closest to Conchita and his departure was very painful:

"I gave him my blessing and I encouraged him to stay there, charging him with prayers and tears that Christ be everything to him. My heart was torn apart, but no one could understand that. Some people who were visiting me were playing the piano in the living room and so as to not let on, I just stood there acting happy.

"When the time came for the train to depart, I cried a great deal and I prayed a lot. There was not a single soul that could comprehend how I felt or accompany me in this sorrow. I felt so alone. Oh, Jesus, may you be blessed! Receive my sacrifice on behalf of my son, this soul so beloved, and may your will be done, not mine."

On November 27th, she received a letter from Manuel notifying her that he had been accepted into the Society of Jesus and that he was about to begin his novitiate. Conchita wrote in her diary: "Crying, I gave thanks to God and I read the letter to him on my knees. I had expected this and I had prayed for it, but nevertheless, no matter how hard I tried, my heart cried and beat with all tenderness."

Fifteen years later, Manuel was ordained a priest in Manresa, Spain. Upon receiving this news, Conchita wrote: "Dearest God of my heart! How can I repay you? Me, the mother of a priest! How I would like to go to Spain to enjoy the greatest joy that can exist on earth! I would love to see him ascend to the altar, see him bring down Jesus into his hands, receive Communion from him. My God, help me to offer up this desire, and pay no attention to the tears which flow from my eyes beyond my control."

Maybe some think that Conchita would act strangely after having received such extraordinary graces, but that was not so. On the contrary, all who knew her have said that her most apparent characteristic was simplicity and good will toward all.

Allow me to relate this anecdote that I heard from the lips of Father Ramón del Real. Conchita herself told him this:

There was one afternoon when Conchita was waiting for a trolley car to go from Coyoacán to San Ángel. She had been waiting, standing there for more than half an hour and the trolley had not arrived.... In the distance, there appeared a cart drawn by three donkeys which was empty and Conchita thought, "If the trolley does not arrive, I will go by donkey...."

"'Pardon me sir! By any chance, are you going to San Ángel?'"

"'Yes, madam, I will be passing by there.'"

"'I am going that way. Would you allow me to ride your little donkey, because the trolley has not arrived?'

"'Very well...this one is the tamest.'"

And Conchita went along very contentedly to San Ángel mounted on a donkey, telling the good man about the times when she was young and lived in her mother's hacienda: "On that hacienda, we had a handsome donkey and I liked to ride him. His name was 'Pretty Boy'...."

When this happened, Conchita had already received the transforming union and the mystical incarnation.

FIFTH PERIOD

1907 - 1909

In 1907, Conchita was 45 years old. Of the nine children to whom she had given birth, six were still under her care. The oldest was 21 and the youngest was 8.

Conchita was not poor, but she was a widow who had to be prudent in financial matters. Upon his death, her husband had left her a modest inheritance of 45,000 pesos in the form of railroad stocks. Her son, Francisco, helped her with his income earned working at Boker's hardware store. This was all the family had to meet expenses such as schooling, clothing, illness, food, housing – in short, life with all its necessities.

We can clearly observe something very interesting from Conchita's spiritual itinerary: even though she had received the ultimate mystical graces and reached sublime levels in her prayer life, she still had her minor human defects and the need to continue struggling against these faults. We cannot think, then, that the "purgative way" or the road to purification will someday come to an end. Rather, the reality is that we continue on this path parallel to the illuminative way and the unitive way. This does not end until death, even for those who have achieved authentic holiness.

On January 9, 1907, Conchita wrote to her spiritual director: "In truth, I should admit that I exaggerate; I am giddy and indiscreet. I am not a good mother to my six children. I am extremely passionate about certain things, like a volcano, and about others I am apathetic. There is no middle ground with me. I am more heart than head and for this reason, sometimes I am vehement about certain matters and at other times cold and indifferent. I am fire and ice. I am weak and inconsistent in my mortification; I am tempestuous; in short...I am a wretch."

In her *Account of Conscience* (March 1908), she said that she had "temptations for human love and affection."

God does not ask us for complete perfection, but rather, for a total surrender. And in this matter, indeed, Conchita did not fail. That is why God continued to work in her.

In her *Account of Conscience*, Conchita described how throughout 1907 she experienced "new levels of humility," "new grades of love," and "new forms of prayer." All of this is very interesting for the study of mysticism. But for the purpose of this book, we are going to look at a grace that Conchita received on February 2nd of that year, on the feast of the Presentation of the Lord in the Temple. On that day Jesus spoke to Conchita:

"The mystery that is celebrated today defines your mission, which is to offer constantly to the Father, as a pure victim, the Incarnate Word for the sake of the world. Mary offered me at the temple, she offered me to the Father every day of her life, and she offered me on the Cross. You, too, should always offer me to the eternal Father, just as a priest does on the altar. This is your mission, this is your role in the Church: to offer yourself and all that you have in union with the great Victim."

From then on, Conchita would refer several times to February 2nd as "her day" and that "this should be the mystery that would occupy her entire life." On February 2nd, 1911, the Lord spoke to her again in a similar manner: "The aim of the mystical incarnation is that you offer me to the Father within your heart and that you do this constantly, as an atoning victim, to hold back divine justice and obtain many graces of salvation for the world."

This will be the essence of the Spirituality of the Cross and it will be fulfilled in the exercise of the "Chain of Love," which we will soon explain.

On March 19th, 1907, Concha, who was then seventeen, told her mother that she wished to enter the Oasis of the Religious of the

68

Cross. Naturally, Conchita was very happy with her daughter's decision, but on August 17th, she wrote in her diary: "I see her full of vanity. The world is attracting her. She thinks she is invulnerable to marriage, but I think she will fall in love with the first young man who comes around. What can I do? I will be vigilant and wait."

The next day Concha told her mother that she no longer wished to enter the Oasis. Soon after that she began to receive various love letters, as she was indeed a very beautiful young lady.

But surprisingly, in April of 1908, Concha clearly felt that her vocation was not matrimony, but rather the religious life. She asked to be admitted to the Oasis. Conchita wrote: "If this is her decision, I will see in it the will of God. I believe that she will go to the retreat tomorrow and perhaps she will never leave the convent again.

"In regard to my faith, I am very happy. But my heart is made of flesh and I feel intense pain. Dear God, give me the strength to hand her over to you without any reservations. I already know the many accusations that will come my way – all the things my own family will say about me. But let your will be done here on earth as it is in heaven."

On April 19th, which was Easter Sunday, Concha entered the convent as a postulant. Conchita wrote: "I turned her over completely to the Mother Superior and the Mistress of Novices. And now this role has surely ended for me. I prayed for a while in the chapel and I came out smiling, but with a deep pain in my heart."

Just as Conchita had predicted, the criticisms soon began. In her biography, she related the names they called her: "the cruel one" and the "mother without a heart." They said that she had influenced her daughter and forced her to join. They made many other false accusations, which Conchita "offered up to the Lord."

It is worthwhile to note here that Conchita's children were completely unaware of the spiritual wealth of their mother. They knew nothing about her writings, of her intervention on behalf of the

Works of the Cross, of her acts of penitence, of her nocturnal prayers and even less of the mystical gifts and graces she had received from the Lord. To them, Conchita was simply a good mother and a devout Christian who liked to go to Mass every day, unless one of the children was ill or she herself was sick. They knew nothing more. It was only after her death that they slowly began to discover the reality of who this admirable woman was.

Two years later, Concha made her vows as a Sister of the Cross. Her mother attended the ceremony and since the ritual refers to the elect as a "Spouse of Christ," Conchita graciously commented, "Now it can be said that Jesus is my son-in-law."

On her birthday, December 8th, Conchita went to spend the day in retreat at the house of the Sisters of the Poor. At noon they brought her meal, but she had observed that there was a very poor hut nearby and without anybody noticing it, she took her food to the people who were living inside the cottage:

"There was a poor man near death lying on a mat and a woman grinding something I did not recognize. I felt nauseous and filled with repugnance, but Jesus helped me to overcome these feelings. I gave them my meal and I sat down to talk with them by the doorway. They put the plates that I had brought them on top of a dirty crate, the only piece of furniture in the hut, and they began to eat with much gratitude. How good are the poor! No wonder the memory of their misery does not allow me to sleep when it gets cold. I gave them some alms and I departed. I want to continue helping this family that our Lady has given to me today. "

Those who knew Conchita said that, although she didn't have much, she was very generous with the poor and that many came to her door to ask for a simple "taco," some alms, or some clothing. They knew she would never turn them away.

Ever since Jesus said, "whatever you do to the least of mine, you do to me," there can never exist an authentic Christian spirituality without a sincere concern for the poor. For this reason, in all the constitutions and rules of congregations and religious institutes, there should be some articles that explicitly regulate almsgiving and social assistance. Anything to the contrary would be neither Christian rules, nor Christian institutions.

At this time, we cannot continue discussing Conchita's personal life, because that is not the purpose of this book. For that reason, we now look at what occurred on October 24th, 1909. During that month, the Lord spoke to Conchita regarding a new association. She noted, The Lord spoke of THE COVENANT OF LOVE for several days and on the 24th, he gave me the by-laws for this association. This is what he said:

"I want an association of lay people that is spiritually connected to the Oasis, but is nevertheless independent. It will include appropriate guidelines so that the members can lead a holy life in their homes.

"Who can penetrate and understand the depths of my love for the world, which is so often lost for lack of sacrificial love. For that reason, I have told you that this is a work of salvation and that it will be vast."

Conchita first communicated this to Archbishop of Puebla, Ramón Ibarra, to see what he would think of it. Archbishop liked this idea very much. He studied it, gave it canonical form and approved the association for his diocese on November 3rd. Five days later, the first small group of the Covenant of Love began its work in Puebla.

On November 12th, the Archbishop of Mexico City, José Mora y del Rio, also approved this association for his diocese and the first small group in this city was formed on the 30th. And in six months the group had become quite large. It met in the Chapel of the Oasis. On May 26th, 1910, Conchita wrote in her diary: "Today I felt a deep and holy emotion. I went to listen to the sermon delivered to the Covenant at the Chapel of the Oasis, but there was no room inside for me. Nevertheless I was filled with joy seeing so many members wearing their medals."

On November 15th, 1909, Conchita began to write the *Manual for the Covenant of Love,* which was printed on June 18th, 1910. "It actually turned out pretty well," Conchita commented in her diary.

Like the Apostolate of the Cross, this ministry has evolved greatly over the course of the years. I will quote a few passages from the group's current by-laws to help explain the Spirituality of the Cross.

The Covenant of Love with the Sacred Heart of Jesus is one of the five Works of the Cross, established in the Church to promote following Christ as Priest and Victim.

These five works constitute, in their totality, THE WORKS OF THE CROSS, which is one entity, because each work upholds the same spirituality. The five works represent different expressions of the same spirituality, each defined by the nature and state of life of its members.

The members of the Covenant of Love are to be secular men and women who have achieved a certain level of spiritual maturity, who live a solid Christian life and who have the capacity to make a firm commitment to a life filled with a sense of community and apostolic action. They should also have sufficient knowledge of the Spirituality of the Cross and be living that reality in their daily lives.

The incorporation into Christ through baptism initiates our transformation into him and makes us participants in his priesthood. The Spirituality of the Cross commits us to live out this baptismal priesthood as a means of following Christ 'who through the Holy Spirit offered himself as an immaculate sacrifice to God' (He 9:14).

Baptismal priesthood leads us to identify with Christ as Victim, being that he has already lived his priesthood as a continual and total self-oblation to the Father for the good of humankind.

The exercise of this baptismal call leads us to live in an intimate relationship with the Father, offering Jesus to him and offering ourselves along with Jesus, for the good of the Church and of the world, because the sacrifice of his Son is the only one that will please him and thus save humanity.

Christ manifests his love for the Father by making himself completely available to him, 'obedient even unto death on the Cross' (Phil 2:8). In order to imitate Christ, we shall search for the will of the Father in everything and we will live the filial attitude that Jesus manifested upon saying, 'I have come to do your will' (He 10:7).

Called to transform ourselves into Christ as Priest, holy, innocent, without blemish, we should live in a constant struggle against personal and social sin in all of its manifestations. We will seek an increasing purification, in order to reach a holy life pleasing to God.

Through this union with Jesus, we make our lives a permanent offering to the Father, by which we shall embrace the cross with generosity each day. We shall strive to live an austere life, filled with evangelical poverty, and we shall make whatever sacrifices love inspires us to do.

In his prayers, Jesus sought a continual intimacy with his Father and a fervent intercession for all of us, his brothers and sisters. We will imitate him by constant prayer, which is our path to identify and unite ourselves to him as we praise the Father and intercede for our brethren, especially for our Priests.

As laity, we shall seek that balance between intense prayer and the fulfillment of the duties of our state in life.

The Eucharist makes Christ present as a priestly offering. For that reason, we should participate in it consciously and actively, uniting our own oblation with that of Jesus.

To live within the Mystery of Christ, we should base our spiritual life on the liturgical year of the Church.

Jesus 'humbled himself and took the form of a slave' (Phil 2:7). We should live that priestly attitude of Christ, recognizing our misery and insignificance before God and practicing meekness and understanding in our service to our brothers and sisters.

In this work, the dimension of community is a fundamental element. It leads us to share our personal reality, our prayer and our apostolic action as brothers and sisters.

To be a sign and leaven of unity amid the People of God, we shall seek all means to promote communion with our brethren at all levels.

Christ as Priest offered himself in order to give glory to his Father through the salvation of all humanity.

As members of the Covenant of Love, called to participate in this priestly mystery, we should generously commit ourselves to this work of salvation through the testimony of our lives, through our prayer, through our sacrifice and through our apostolic action.

It is a characteristic of the Covenant of Love that its members live their consecration to God as lay people, through their commitment to sanctify earthly existence and restore all things in Christ. They should promote the human and Christian values of family and of different states of life within the world. They should, with a Christian perspective, work constantly to better the conditions of human life, especially among those most in need.

The field of action for the lay person in his or her apostolic endeavor should encompass all aspects of human life. In so doing, we seek to modify the structures of human life to be in accordance with the requirements of the Gospel.

The supreme manifestation of Christ's priestly love was the giving of his life for humanity. To follow him, we shall take up our cross daily by fulfilling the duties of our state in life and generously giving of ourselves to help our brethren. Thus we shall 'fill up in our flesh what is still lacking in regard to Christ's afflictions, for the sake of his body, which is the Church.'

To consecrate our world to God, we shall collaborate with our activities, career or work, in the Christian renewal of the temporal order in the world and within human structures. We shall actively cooperate with an evangelical spirit in carrying out our daily social, cultural, political and economic functions.

We will try to create a consciousness of the social dimension of sin. And in the light of the social doctrine of the Church, we will participate in the liberation of humanity, especially of those who suffer the consequences of injustice in our world. We shall strive to establish social structures that promote respect for human dignity.

In our apostolic action and in the spreading of the Spirituality of the Cross, we should have the same attitude as Christ, giving, as he did, preference to the poorest and neediest members of our society.

Our transformation into Christ as Priest and Victim implies we imitate him in his love for the Father and for all brethren, even unto death. Moved by the Holy Spirit, we shall endeavor to create in ourselves that attitude of total self-giving to the Father and to others.

SIXTH PERIOD

1910 - 1913

On August 2nd, 1910, Conchita's oldest son got married. As a wedding gift, she gave her son a watch that had belonged to his father along with this letter:

I want to give you not just one blessing, but a thousand blessings, on this day.

You have been a model son and I hope that you will be as Christian, as dignified, as loving, and as noble a husband as your father was. This way you will please your wife, Elisa, who with such love and goodness will unite her destiny to yours. She should be the center of your happiness, the one who will make a proper home for you and who will be the mother of your children. Respect her, love her and hold her in the highest esteem, so that she will be what you want her to be.

Avoid all conflict and, to preserve the peace, never hesitate to make any sacrifice for her. With prudence, good manners and a little flexibility, you will avoid many problems.

Treat Elisa with all sweetness, preferring to use persuasion and reason to win her over rather than force and authoritarianism, which will only cool love. The greatest danger to a marriage is to put out the flame of love, respect, and mutual esteem. That is why whenever you are angry, hold your tongue and you will never regret it.

Do not bring your friends to your home too often. And neither should you fall into the hateful trap of jealousy, because husbands who do not trust have very little respect for their own dignity and that of their spouse.

Continue being a dignified person. Never soil your soul with dirty business affairs that defraud your neighbor and you will be happy. Poverty itself never stains nor dishonors.

Never spend more than you have or all that you have. Taking care of your finances will avoid many problems in your marriage.

May the care of the poor be one of your regular expenses and God will never fail you.

Do not measure your faith by exterior acts, but rather by the practice of the virtues. However, keep in mind that practices of piety, even those that appear insignificant, are very important in the formation of the family.

Forgive me, my son, for all the bad examples I have shown you. Never follow them.

I bless you again in your father's name and in mine. Be happy in your marriage. You will be, if you obey the will of God and you place it in the center of your heart.

Your mother, who loves and blesses you...

Conchita then wrote to her daughter Concha, who was a nun: "Pray to God that I may be a good mother-in-law. I am afraid that I might not be a good one."

On January 19th, 1912, God inspired Conchita with the idea of the fourth Work of the Cross, "The Apostolic League," dedicated to priests. This organization of service, now called "The Fraternity of Christ the Priest," invites priests to fully live the spirituality of Jesus as Priest and Victim. It also invites priests to fraternize with other priests.

To this date, this work has experienced little growth. But I believe that if this work takes root in the hearts of the clergy, it will be an enormous blessing for the Church. In essence, it deals with planting and cultivating the seed of the sublime truth within all priests that not only are they called by God to offer the Divine Victim, but that they are to be themselves an offering, a victim without blemish, in union with Christ. Given that Christ is both Priest and Victim, we cannot imagine following Christ as a priest without also following him as victim.

On March 23rd, Conchita had the opportunity to go to Puebla to talk with Archbishop Ibarra regarding the Apostolic League. The holy bishop became very enthusiastic about this work and soon he gave it his approval. He sent out a flyer to be printed entitled "The Apostolic League," in which he outlined a general idea of the principles of this work. He sent a copy to all of the bishops of the Republic of Mexico, along with a letter in which he invited them to join this organization and asked them to indicate other people in their diocese who could be invited to join as well. Four archbishops and ten bishops gave their enthusiastic approval to the work and signed up to be members.

Archbishop Ibarra drew up a "draft of statutes" of this work and sent it to the interested bishops.

A year later, the Apostolic League numbered fourteen bishops and two hundred seventy-nine priests. And on December 13th, 1913, Pope Pius X granted abundant indulgences for those who would associate themselves with this work.

The religious persecution of 1914 and the subsequent death of Archbishop Ibarra on February 1st, 1917, almost completely halted the activity and progress of the Apostolic League. Currently, it is being restructured under its new title, Fraternity of Christ the Priest.

Since 1904, Conchita had been thinking about the founding of the Religious Men of the Cross and about Father Felix Rougier's return so that he could take over this task. But the years had passed and there seemed to be no hope that this would happen.

Various Mexican bishops had written letters and made trips to Rome and France to obtain permission for the founding of this group and for the return of Father Felix to Mexico, but they had had no success. The reason for the opposition was that this matter was based on the revelations of a certain Mrs. Concepción Cabrera and in these cases the ecclesiastical authorities acted with great caution.

Conchita suffered much because of this. In her diary, we read: "If you want the whole world to think I am deluded and that I am a meddler, then I want that also. If you want me to see your Works of the Cross, which mean so much to me, destroyed before my very eyes, I will accept this sacrifice with all my heart. If you want to see me mocked by all who know me, for your love I want that also. If you want those who used to support me, to now abandon me so that I remain alone, embracing your cross, I shall not hesitate to drink of this chalice, only because I love you."

Some months later, Conchita wrote: "All the doors are now shutting. I don't even know if Father Felix is alive. I have seen a thousand expectations perish before my eyes, hopes and dreams that had nourished my life. I cry and I wait; this is how the days, the months and the years go by. And as I see my dreams burst like soap bubbles, in my soul only disillusion and discouragement remain…."

Without a doubt, God wanted to cleanse Conchita of every last bit of attachment to anything that was not of God himself, even if they were holy and good things. For it happens to all of us that, almost without realizing it and due to our enthusiasm, we end up wanting to accomplish certain good works just to satisfy ourselves. We do not seek purely to do God's will. Thus our hearts are bound; we lack self-giving and fail to be at the disposal of the hands of God.

That is why Conchita wrote this prayer: "Receive what I am about to tell you, my Lord, and give me the strength to fulfill it. Today, with all my strength, I yank the "Religious Men of the Cross" from my soul. I want to rip them from my heart. I sacrifice my wishes to your will and I offer to never, ever, talk about this group again except with you. I will talk about them with others only if you desire it.

"I lay aside all hopes that this or that person might accomplish the founding of this work. I offer this desire as a sacrifice forever.

"I also turn each and every one of my children over to you. They are yours. Do with them what you will."

That is how Conchita began to liberate her soul of all selfish desires and began emptying her heart so as to fill it solely with God.

Archbishop of Puebla, Ramón Ibarra, had been one of those who most supported the founding of the Religious Men of the Cross. That is why he decided to ask Conchita's permission to allow certain theologians to examine her and then send their conclusions to Rome. Conchita humbly put herself at the disposal of the Archbishop and was examined by Fathers Leandro Laidy, a Lazarist, Tomás Ipiña, a Jesuit provincial, Alejandro Cepeda, a Claretian and Carlos M. Mayer, a Jesuit. For an entire month, these priests interviewed Conchita separately and read her writings. Later they turned over their evaluations to the Archbishop of Mexico, José Mora y del Río. After reading them, he sent them to Archbishop Ibarra, who happened to be in Mexico around that time. He told him that the unanimous conclusion was very favorable. They concluded that, in reality, all was from God. So he was disposed to write once again to Rome on behalf of the three Archbishops of Mexico (Mora, Ibarra and Ruiz) asking for the founding of the Religious Men of the Cross.

The day Archbishop Ibarra told her the good news, Conchita wrote in her diary: "I feel like a donkey that has come upon an alfalfa feed lot and as I have received so many beatings to get to this point, I approach it with fear, thinking this is not meant for me...poor beast!"

At the beginning of January 1910, Archbishop Ibarra went to Rome to present the judgments of the examiners. He also took the

Constitutions of the Religious Men of the Cross, which had been written by Conchita and Father Felix Rougier in 1904. Cardinal Vives, who was in charge of such affairs, examined the papers and gave his approval. He presented his opinion to Pope Pius X, feeling assured that the Holy Father would approve the foundation. However, Pope Pius X asked that the whole matter be examined further and more thoroughly. On March 2nd, the Pope wrote the following letter to Archbishop Ibarra in his own handwriting:

> Venerable brother: I have read your letter in which you lament the delay of approval for the establishment of the Congregation of the Priests of the Cross. I beg you to forgive me, as well as the Sacred Congregation of Religious, for believing that in such a serious matter we should proceed cautiously before giving it approval. However, I assure you that this matter will promptly be submitted to the Sacred Congregation for their study and God willing, it will be resolved in accordance with your wishes and those of your brothers in Christ.

> Be confident, then, because a work that is pleasing to the Lord, even though it may encounter many difficulties, will never be defeated by any one obstacle. With this hope, my venerable brother, I give you my apostolic blessing with all my heart. (Pope Pius X, Rome, March 2, 1910)

Archbishop Ibarra returned to his diocese. After a year and a half, he still had not heard from Rome. Finally, he received a letter from Father Carmelo Blay, informing him that the consultants of the Sacred Congregation of the Religious had already turned in their vote regarding Conchita's writings and the solicited approval of the Congregation of the Religious of the Cross. Thus, Archbishop Ibarra again wrote to the Pope to remind him of the matter dealing with the founding of the Congregation. This letter is dated July 4th, 1911, and is signed by five archbishops and seven bishops of the Republic of Mexico.

On August 17th, Cardinal Rodolfo Caroli responded:

"I received your letter in which you recommend the founding of the Priests of the Cross. This is something that I can attend to directly, since at the Sacred Congregation I am in charge of the religious institutions for men. The religious authorities who recommend the approval of this application are held in the highest esteem. But even so, and considering past antecedents, I perceive that success will not be easily obtained, at least at this time. I will certainly do everything possible on my part to obtain what is desired."

A year went by without any news. Archbishop Ibarra then wrote to Cardinal Caroli: "It has been quite a while since the Roman consultants named to examine Mrs. Concepción Cabrera's writings turned in their results to the Sacred Congregation of the Religious. To date, nothing has been resolved. I believe the time has come for you to do us the favor of moving on this issue so that the approval of the founding of the Priests of the Cross can be obtained as soon as possible" (Mexico, October 22, 1912).

Cardinal Caroli responded: "Regarding the Priests of the Cross, I do not think this founding will be permitted. The writings in question, your Excellency, are being examined, and from what I can deduce, the truth is that one cannot currently speak of a founding. Therefore, there is nothing to be done at this time."

During that time, Jesus again spoke to Conchita about the Priests of the Cross and he told her: "The Priests of the Cross will soon come to crown the Works."

Conchita answered, "That is what you always tell me, my beautiful Jesus, but look at all the delays."

Then, at last, it was 1913. During this year, Conchita's nest was almost empty. Of her nine children, two had died, two had entered the religious life, one had married and two were in boarding school, studying in Puebla. Only two were living with her: twenty year-old Ignacio, who worked in his brother Pancho's office, and eighteen-year-old Pablo, who was attending a Jesuit college.

On June 17th, Pablo returned home with a very high fever. Two days later, he vomited blood and the doctor's diagnosis was that he had a grave case of typhus. They called Father Pedro Jimenez so that Pablo could make his general confession. The confessor was there only a few minutes and when he came out he said to Conchita, "Don't ask God for Pablo's recovery; let him go to heaven. He's very innocent. He is a pure soul; he's a child. I think this is how God wants him."

Conchita's diary details those days:

"June 24th: Pablo is still very sick. I don't want to separate myself from him, not even one instant. I am without servants and with no one to accompany me with my sick son. He sets admirable examples for me. He often repeats, 'My God, may your will be done.'

"I asked him: 'What do you want – to be healed or to go to heaven?'

"'Well, to go to heaven.'

"'Why?'

"'To see Jesus. And to give the Holy Virgin a thousand kisses. And after I have arrived there, I'll ask God to give me permission to come and give you a kiss.'

"I lent him my crucifix and he frequently prays, kissing it.

"Suddenly, he told me: "'I will not be here for my saint's feast day (June 29th). I feel very bad and the medicines are doing nothing for me. Mother, I don't think that I have been a bad person. I've only had good friends and I haven't even been to the movies. I'm leaving clean...'

"June 25th: He doesn't recognize me anymore. I was beside him and he shouted, 'I want my mother! Call my mother.' I can't

84

explain what I felt. I started crying. Sometimes, one cannot understand what he says. He never closes his gorgeous blue eyes. Today he fixed his eyes on me. I have his gaze imprinted on my soul.

"June 26th: He is on his deathbed. My Pablo is leaving me! He's so humble. He always had the least, the oldest of things; those things that had belonged to others. We all bossed him around and gladly he obeyed. He was as pure as an angel, bearing all of his illnesses without complaining. He was so patient, so prudent. He went through this life, unappreciated, as the last one in everything, and without being able to do anything about it. It was his journey, the journey of the saints. My God, my soul is tearing! Oh God of my heart, I unite my will to yours, but my heart – a mother's heart – is breaking. Mother of mine, help me!

"June 27th: A day of pain as a mother and a day of happiness as a Christian. Today I surrendered Pablo to Jesus. Very few people have interrupted my solitude due to fear of getting typhus. Salvador and Guadalupe arrived from Puebla, but they found their brother already dead. Close to midnight, I went to sleep a little…

"June 29th: I became sick and was bedridden. Today is the feast day of my two sons who are in heaven, Pedro and Pablo. My God, please congratulate them for me. Mary, my good Mother, do give them a kiss for me. I got up to go to Mass; however, I felt very bad. God seems to want me more and more alone. So be it, that I may serve as I should – to pray and to work for his glory."

Two months went by and the Archbishop of Puebla had a new initiative in favor of the Works of the Cross.

Archbishop Ibarra was a determined man. No obstacle ever prevented him from doing what he felt needed to be done. Therefore, he planned to return to Rome to obtain the approval of the foundation of the Religious Men of the Cross. This time, however, he intended to take the stumbling block – Conchita – with him. He also decided to bring two new assessments of great authority concerning Conchita. One of these was from Archbishop Maximino Ruiz, who had been

Conchita's spiritual director from 1905 to 1911, and who had just been named Bishop of San Cristobal de las Casas. The other was from Father Poulain, a famous Jesuit, who had written a "Treatise on Mystical Theology."

Archbishop Ibarra organized a pilgrimage to the Holy Land and to Rome. He managed to bring together one hundred twenty-three pilgrims. Among this group were two bishops and thirty-three priests. The rest were laity, including Conchita and two of her children, Nacho and Lupe.

The pilgrimage en route to Palestine left Mexico on August 26th, 1913. Conchita wrote many pages about her impressions, as she visited the places where Jesus was born, lived, preached and died for us and for our salvation.

Later, as they were approaching Rome, her prayers intensified and so did her fears, because she knew that in Rome the definitive battle for the founding of the Priests of the Cross would be fought.

The pilgrims arrived in Rome on November 13th. Archbishop Ibarra arranged for a private audience with Pope Saint Pius X. He was granted the audience on the 17th for himself and for the "famous" Mrs. Cabrera.

Conchita said that when she was told of the private audience, she froze; and during the five days before the event, that she did special prayers and special penances.

On the day of the meeting, Archbishop Ibarra spoke first, alone with the Holy Father. After that, Conchita entered. Let her words speak for themselves:

"I can't describe the emotion that I felt. The Pope was sitting at his desk. In front of him was Archbishop Ibarra. I knelt before the Pope, and crying, kissed his feet. Finally, I composed myself and he asked me what it was that I wanted.

"'That Your Holiness approve the Priests of the Cross,' I told him without letting go of his hand, which he had stretched out for me to kiss.

"'They are approved, and before the end of this year everything regarding this matter will be settled.'

"'Holy Father, I do not want to be an obstacle for the Works of the Cross, and I beg you that I be eliminated from these works, that I not be taken into account, that I be completely omitted, so that the works take on their own course.'

"'I already spoke with Archbishop Ibarra regarding this matter, and everything will be settled this year. What else are you asking of me?'

"'Your blessing for the Sisters of the Cross, the Works of the Cross, and for my children.'

"'Yes, and for you, a very special one, as well.'

"He was looking into my eyes with his penetrating, sweet gaze, and I felt as if I were at the feet of Our Lord. He blessed me and then said, in Italian, 'Pray, pray for me.'

"Then he spoke at length with Archbishop Ibarra. At the end, I heard the Pope tell him that out of obedience he needed to see a doctor and to take care of himself."

Archbishop Ibarra and Conchita left the meeting radiant and happy, praising and thanking God.

On December 7th, Cardinal Donato Sbarretti examined Conchita, speaking for two hours with her about many instances of her life, about her writings and especially about that which was related to the mystical incarnation, for this had stirred up certain doctrinal difficulties. Conchita says that due to this lengthy conversation with Cardinal Sbarretti, many points that had been obscured in the past now became clearer to him.

Finally, on December 18th, Archbishop Ibarra received a letter from Cardinal Sbarretti in which he communicated the Pope's decision:

"I hasten to communicate to you that the Holy Father, in his meeting with His Eminence the Cardinal Prefect on the 16th of the current month, has kindly accepted the petition of Your Excellency and of the rest of the bishops of Mexico, asking for the authority to found a new congregation of men, especially in view of the declaration of Your Excellency that the mentioned institute will not be associated in any way with the presumed revelations of Mrs. Cabrera de Armida. Nonetheless, the Holy Father has set the following conditions, that: (1) the new institute's name will be 'Missionaries of the Holy Spirit,' and (2) the priests Alberto Cusco y Mir and Felix of Jesus Rougier, former spiritual directors of the aforementioned Mrs. Cabrera, never be part of it."

But why did Pius X change his mind?

It is evident that before the audience, he had been very well informed regarding the status of the situation that he was to discuss with Archbishop Ibarra. Now there were four new opinions that weighed in favor of the founding of the Priests of the Cross:

Bishop Maximino Ruiz' account was one of those testimonies. He had been Conchita's spiritual director for six years. Bishop Ruiz' account of Conchita was based solely on her actual life and Christian virtues. He especially mentioned her profound humility, her extraordinary purity, her consistent charity toward the poor and the loyalty she displayed in meeting her obligations as a mother and as a head of household. Bishop Ruiz was applying the infallible measure that Jesus left us so that we would be able to discern the true prophets from the false ones. By its fruits one knows a tree and by his actions one knows a man. "One does not harvest grapes from the bramble or gather figs from the thorns: Therefore, by their actions you will be able to know them" (Mt 7:16).

The second factor was Father Poulain's prudent theological judgment, which was very favorable. The third one was Archbishop Ibarra's petition, which was that the Congregation of the Priests of the Cross be founded based on its own worth, its benefit to Mexico and disentangled from Conchita's revelations. Lastly, without a doubt, the insistence of many very dignified bishops weighed in significantly; this had to be taken into consideration. Cardinal Sbarretti's evaluation of Conchita and of some of her writings may have served as another point in its favor.

Archbishop Ibarra had his last audience with Pope Pius X on December 22nd. This was to thank him and to say goodbye. In this audience, Archbishop asked the Pope how the condition that Father Felix Rougier would not be a part of the new institute should be interpreted. The Pope made it clear that the intention was that Father Felix should not leave his congregation in order to enter into the Congregation of the Missionaries of the Holy Spirit, but that he could help form the new priests of this new congregation until they would be able to govern themselves. Obviously, this would happen only with his Superior General's permission and under the conditions that he would permit.

So ended the mission to Rome. Now Archbishop Ibarra and Conchita had to go forward to France, to the city of Lyon, to solicit the permission of the Superior General of the Marist Priests for Father Felix Rougier.

SEVENTH PERIOD

1914 - 1916

Archbishop Ibarra and Conchita arrived in the city of Lyon, France, on January 3rd, 1914. It was where Father Juan Raffin, Superior General of the Marist Fathers, was assigned.

Archbishop Ibarra was insistent and pleaded with Father Raffin to give Father Felix the desired permission to go to Mexico to take charge of the foundation of the Missionaries of the Holy Spirit. But Father Raffin, after consulting with his Advisory Board, told Archbishop Ibarra that, due to a lack of personnel, it was impossible to grant that permission. He explained that the shortage of Marist priests was so great that the Board had decided to close the school they had in Mexico City. Therefore, the negative response was a definitive one.

There was thus nothing left to do there. So it was that Archbishop Ibarra and his small number of followers took the train to Paris to begin their return trip to Mexico.

They arrived in Paris on the 9th and on that day Conchita received an unexpected visit at the hotel. It was Mr. Jorge Greville and his wife, Isabel. Father Felix had been their director for many years. Due to this relationship, the Grevilles had been informed of everything regarding the Works of the Cross. Hence, they went to meet Conchita. She and Archbishop Ibarra explained to them the problem regarding the permission for Father Felix, and the Grevilles agreed to go to see Father Raffin. They were dear friends of Father Raffin, so they wanted to visit him to find out if they could help with the situation.

Indeed, they went, met with Father Raffin and won the "fight." Father Raffin gave the desired permission.

How was that possible? Mrs. Isabel Greville found the solution. Given that the problem was a shortage of personnel, she suggested that Archbishop Ibarra lend three priests to the Marist school in Mexico, so that it wouldn't have to close. This would be in exchange for Father Felix's permission to take charge of the foundation of the Missionaries of the Holy Spirit. Father Raffin accepted this immediately and so did Archbishop Ibarra. Thus, everything was resolved.

Father Felix had to finish the school year and right after that he traveled to Mexico. He disembarked in Veracruz on August 14th. The Mexican Revolution, which lasted from 1910 to 1917, was at its height.

The next day, as General Obregon's troops took Mexico City, Father Felix arrived in Puebla, looking for Archbishop Ibarra. But he was in Mexico City, well hidden in a private home due to the religious persecution. This persecution had gotten quite out of hand since June of that year. Many priests were in prison and many had been shot; others were driven into exile. Sisters were driven out of their convents. The churches were profaned and shut down. Public worship was prohibited. Seminaries and all Church properties were confiscated.

Father Felix was in Puebla more than a month, in a private home, where his brothers, the Marists, lived in hiding.

It was not until October 24th that Father Felix was able to travel to Mexico City with sufficient safety. On that same day, he met Conchita in her own home. It had been ten years since they had seen each other or communicated with each other. The first few words of Father Felix were, "I have not changed in regard to the Works of the Cross."

The Marists had a school in Mexico City called Colegio Franco Inglés and thanks to the personal intervention of the Minister of Public Education, the school was able to remain open. It was here that Father Felix stayed and he and Archbishop Ibarra were in constant communication with each other.

Between the two of them, they brought together four young people to be the first novices of this new congregation. On December 25th, the feast of our Savior's birth, the Congregation of the Missionaries of the Holy Spirit was founded at seven in the morning, behind closed doors, in the chapel of "Las Rosas," which is at the foot of Tepeyac Hill.

In attendance were Archbishop Ibarra, Conchita, Father Felix, two of the four postulants, the owners of the chapel and a few other people. A Mass was celebrated, and the Pontifical Decree that authorized the Foundation was read, as well as the names of the four future novices. Then Archbishop Ibarra gave thanks to God for what had been accomplished so far, despite the many obstacles. He finished by saying: "Therefore, by virtue of the powers conferred on me by the Holy See, I declare canonically open from this moment on, the Novitiate of the Congregation of the Missionaries of the Holy Spirit."

Then, directing himself to the two postulants, he said: "Father Felix, present with us today, will be the Master of Novices. Respect him, love him and obey him. He will teach you the true spirit of the Cross and will make good religious of you. May God bless you, as I am now giving you my blessing."

After having given his blessing, Archbishop Ibarra returned to his hiding place. One by one, the rest of the people began to come out. They exercised great caution, because at "La Villa" there were always many soldiers.

Near "La Villa," Archbishop Ibarra had a small house that he had bought to shelter the poor pilgrims who would go to the Sanctuary of the Virgin of Guadalupe from his own diocese. He also gladly lent it to become the first novitiate of the Missionaries of the Holy Spirit. This place had no furniture whatsoever, and there for a while, Father Felix and the four novices sat on the floor and ate on some boxes, with the initial happiness and enthusiasm common to those beginning a new endeavor.

As mentioned earlier, the *Constitutions* of the new Congregation had been drafted by Conchita and Father Felix in 1904. In 1910, Cardinal Vives charged Father Felipe Maroto, canonist of the Congregation of the Heart of Mary, to review the Constitution. Father Maroto gave it canonical form. This Constitution was that which governed the last of the Works of the Cross for many years. Naturally, as time went by, the Constitution changed through a process of evolution in order to better adapt to new circumstances, but the spirituality was left untouched. From the present *Constitutions*, I'll quote the following paragraphs to help us better understand the spiritual school that we are studying:

By the divine will, we, the Missionaries of the Holy Spirit, are called to consecrate our lives to God as religious, by radically following Christ, Priest and Victim, with the purpose of transforming ourselves into him.

We will strive to share his priestly feelings and to make his virtues our own, above all his love, purity and sacrifice.

By the power of the Holy Spirit, we are to imitate Jesus in his obedient love for the Father and his humble love for humanity, in order to exercise our spiritual priesthood, offering him and offering ourselves with him, as hosts pleasing to God.

Being aware that only the Holy Spirit can transform us into Christ, we consecrate ourselves to him, and we are to be docile to his action in us.

The Virgin Mary is the perfect model of transformation into Christ, Priest and Victim. We will profess a filial love to her and turn to her constantly for her intercession.

The spirit of the Congregation is lived by offering the Word Incarnate and offering ourselves with him to the Father, through the hands of Mary, for the salvation of the world.

The characteristic manner of living this spirituality is the Chain of Love and its symbol is the Cross of the Apostolate.

Our mission is the same as the mission of Jesus, who was sent to save and sanctify us through the gift of his Spirit.

We live out our radical following of Christ by professing the evangelical virtues of poverty, chastity and obedience.

Contemplation and apostolic action are essential to the nature of our institute. But our prayer life is what is most important of all. It is the source and the fountain of apostolic fruitfulness.

Our mission demands that we be men of prayer, focusing lovingly on God until we reach the point where contemplation is a condition in which prayer dominates our entire lives and our souls are continuously under its influence.

The center of our contemplative dimension is the mystery of Christ, Priest and Victim, which perpetuates and actualizes itself in the Eucharist. Therefore, we are to lead an intense liturgical life which has a most devoted celebration of the Eucharist as its daily climax.

Christ continues his priestly oblation in his true and real presence in each Consecrated Host. Hence, our prayer before the Blessed Sacrament occupies a primary place in our religious life.

The spirit of sacrifice, necessary to imitate the crucified Christ, is characteristic of our life; it is to lead us to a progressive purification, to a capacity for commitment and to true love.

Constant study is to be the nourishment of our contemplative life and a requirement for our apostolate.

The main focus of our apostolate is on the five Works of the Cross and on service to priests and to consecrated souls.

The vocation of the Missionary of the Holy Spirit, then, has two dimensions: One refers to BEING, which consists in a progressive transformation into Christ, Priest and Victim. The other one refers to ACTION and consists in the integral promotion of the laity and its action in the Church, through the Apostleship of the Cross and through the Covenant of Love; and also, of fraternal service to priests, through the Fraternity of Christ the Priest. All of this follows the guidelines of Vatican II.

To continue the story, we will say that once the Church had accepted and taken the five Works of the Cross into her hands, Conchita's external action as founder came to an end. From that point on, her role was that of a mother who offers constant prayers and sacrifices for her children. Moreover, the gift given her of being a teacher and a model for whomever wanted to follow her spirituality, continued throughout her life. Therefore, God continued to enrich her spiritually so that she would fully fulfill this aspect of her vocation.

At the beginning of the year 1914, which is the year we are studying, Archbishop Ibarra obtained permission from the Holy See for Conchita to have a private chapel of the Blessed Sacrament in her home. On March 25th, the chapel with all its necessities was complete. Archbishop Ibarra celebrated Mass there. Thereafter, Jesus remained in that tabernacle.

From that day forward, Conchita's prayer before Jesus in the Blessed Sacrament was more frequent and more intense. That day, she wrote in her diary:

"Oh joyful day! Chosen and fortunate day! Today our good Jesus, merciful Jesus, has deigned to establish his dwelling in my poor house, to cover us with his protective shadow. Oh, my God, why does such a joy come to me that my Lord, my God and my all, has come to dwell with this wretch who deserves nothing? Oh, Jesus, so good and kindhearted, how can I pay back this favor, but by loving you more and more, sacrificing myself for you and dedicating my whole life to you, in holy devotion. May the hours pass, day and night, with this poor sinner at your feet!

"Lord, I am going to tell you something that has been motivated by love: When the world offends you, come here. When someone despises you, come here. When you find nothing but coldness in hearts, come here. Come to your poor Concha (Concha or Conchita, as she was called, means seashell in Spanish), as she will open her arms, her soul, the inner chamber of her heart, the center of all tenderness and she will protect you, as seashells protect their precious pearls. Oh, a thousand times my Beloved, come here! With all my love, I will wipe away your tears; with my kisses, I will heal your wounds and with my soul, my prayers and my penances, I will give you comfort."

To Archbishop Ruiz, she wrote the following: "I have risen to be a sacristan. He is under my watch. I am happy. Like a dog, I sleep guarding my Master's door. When I go to lunch, I invite him; when I go to dinner, I invite him; when I arrive, I greet him. When I leave his tabernacle, I say goodbye with a kiss."

Father Moisés Lira recounted the following anecdote: "One day I went to see Conchita. Immediately, she had me visit the chapel in her home, which had recently been used for the first time. She was so happy that her great sense of humor surfaced and she told me,

'Look at Jesus, how good he is! He is so close to my room that I can even hear him cough…!'"

Prayer before the Blessed Sacrament is a characteristic of the Spirituality of the Cross. In the houses of the Sisters of the Cross and the novitiates of the Missionaries of the Holy Spirit, adoring Jesus in the Blessed Sacrament is a perpetual activity. This is done by taking turns, day and night. There is never an interruption.

In the Constitution of the Missionaries of the Holy Spirit, it is mandated that the members do at least one hour of adoration before Jesus in the tabernacle during the day and, if possible, another hour at night.

In the Apostolate of the Cross and in the Covenant of Love, the laity is invited to adore Jesus in the Blessed Sacrament every day, whenever possible.

Another characteristic of the Spirituality of the Cross is to live a life of faith in intimate union with the Holy Virgin Mary, Mother of Jesus. In this, Conchita is also a model.

"I feel that my love for Mary has grown. It is something new: A new filial tenderness that makes me invoke her often, call upon her and ask her to accompany me, to assist me and to teach me."

Another day, she wrote this: "This afternoon, I experienced a calling from within; it was a necessity to go and see my Jesus and while in prayer, I suddenly felt an unlimited tenderness toward the Mother of Jesus. I felt as if upon turning a corner, I suddenly met her. She is my Mother and she tells me that she knows me and that she always understands. I felt confident, loved and sure of her kindness toward me. How good she is!"

Among the small books she wrote, there is one dedicated to the Virgin Mary, which Conchita entitled: *A Small Bouquet of Loves*, and it contains prayers full of devotion to the Mother of God.

This special devotion to Mary is an integral part of the Spirituality of the Cross; further on, we will see how Mary participates in Jesus' priesthood in a unique way and how she is, before God, the Priestly Mother, the one who received her mission to bear once, and to offer always, the Lamb who takes away the sins of the world.

Here is one last paragraph of the many that Conchita wrote about Mary:

"I want to do everything in union with Mary. That's why I wonder how she would receive the sacrament of the Holy Eucharist; how she would pray; how she would offer her divine Son to the heavenly Father; with how much generosity she would sacrifice for Jesus; how she would live in the presence of God; how many times she would chat with Jesus; how organized she would be; how she would eat; how she would rest as she dreamed about her Jesus; how she would offer advice; how meek and how sweet her words must have been. And thus I want to imitate her more and more. May the Lord deign to help me and may I not live, nor love, nor work by myself, but in union with this Virgin of my soul, this Virgin who is my Blessed Mother."

Those who knew Conchita said that her custom was to always give away rosaries and scapulars in order to sow a devotion to the Mother of Jesus in others.

1915 and 1916 were deplorable years for Mexico. The revolutionary commanders and their troops had divided and were fighting each other for power.

Conchita summarized the situation this way: "A lot of blood has been spilled. Oh my God, what a tremendous punishment! And the ruined businesses…"

Among the ruined establishments was Francisco's business. He was Conchita's oldest son, the married one. His brothers worked with him. But after seeing the terrible situation of the country,

Francisco went to look for work in Brazil, Argentina and New York. If he had managed to establish himself, Ignacio and Salvador would then have also gone to be with him. Conchita wrote: "I don't know what my duty is: should I stay, or go with my sons? Oh, my God, may I know your will and may I accomplish it, even if it crucifies me."

But after eight months of absence and failure, Francisco returned to Mexico.

Meanwhile, in Conchita's house, there was a small revolution going on as well.

"I feel as if I'm a burden to my children. They do not understand me. They are not in agreement with me about many things. I give my opinion, from experience, and they do not value it. When I want something, I am told that people no longer use that...they believe I am foolish..."

Conchita was referring to the three children who still lived under her guardianship: Ignacio, who was twenty-three; Salvador, who was twenty; and Guadalupe, who was eighteen.

Well, we all know that the "generation gap" is more greatly accentuated between parents and their younger children when they reach adolescence and young adulthood. It is natural...and not even the saints escape this problem.

EIGHTH PERIOD

1917 - 1924

On February 1st, 1917, the Archbishop of Puebla, Ramon Ibarra, died. He was the most prominent benefactor and promoter of the Works of the Cross. For a long time, he had suffered from a sore on his foot that occasionally threatened to become gangrenous. In addition, he had diabetes and other complications. When his illnesses became more serious, he traveled to Mexico City to see his doctor and stayed in Conchita's home. There, he died a holy death. He had provided Mrs. Cabrera with spiritual direction and support for four years. His death represented a great loss and an enormous sorrow for Conchita.

Five days after the death of Archbishop Ibarra, Conchita wrote: "I was praying, resigned and abandoned to the will of God, when the Lord told me, 'What is left for you to do is to live the last stage of your life. Please understand your role well. Imitate the virtues of my Mother in her loneliness when I ascended into heaven, while she stayed in the world. Then, my Mother's union with me grew deeper; her adhesion to my will and her longing for heaven grew as well.'"

Conchita further commented: "More than ever before, I need to be more humble. I should be God's servant and a servant to others. I want to hide from everyone's gaze. I want, finally, in these last stages of my life, to do what I am supposed to do: to have an interior life more contemplative in nature and to dedicate my life totally to God and to my duties – all for his greater glory. I am now on the right path, my Mother; show me how to imitate you."

One day, Conchita asked the Lord:

"'Why didn't you take your Mother to heaven on the day of your Ascension? Why did you leave her so alone in the world?'

"'It was because she had not finished her mission as Mother of the Church. She lived to give testimony to my humanity. She lived to be an instrument of the Holy Spirit in the early life of the Church, to live as co-redemptrix and protector, a refuge for her children. She lived to obtain the graces of salvation for everyone, as her maternal instincts demanded it. With the pain of my absence, with the martyrdom of her solitude which she accepted with love, my Mother obtained graces for everyone. Now it is time that people show their appreciation for her.'"

On June 11, the Lord announced to Conchita, "You are going to experience the sufferings of my Mother; the feelings in your heart will echo her pain."

This painful experience lasted eight years, from June 1917 until June 1925. It consisted of a long "night of the soul" in which Conchita experienced a painful "absence of Jesus," a "silence of Jesus," a great internal solitude. And at times the Lord would give her some consolation, giving her new insights, or having her briefly experience his presence and his love.

After the death of Archbishop Ibarra, Conchita chose Bishop Valverde as her spiritual director. He did not take much interest in her. During these years, the Lord repeatedly asked her to simplify her spiritual life and organize it around only one thing: uniting her will totally to the will of God.

"'Simplify your spirit by concretizing your spiritual life in such a way that your will shall be one with mine. Only in this unity of wills is the perfection of love found. One of the errors of creatures consists in multiplying their actions both outwardly and inwardly, instead of simplifying themselves in God, making themselves ONE with God, uniting their will and desires with God's will and desires. How much would souls progress in their spiritual life if they would only take this path – the shortest to achieve sanctification!

"'Do not take yourself into account; rather confidently fling yourself into this unification, in which you will find fulfillment. Die

102

to your will and live in mine. To have one will is to have one love. Love brings unity to perfection.'"

Within a short time, Conchita experienced the change that the Lord wanted to work in her: "I see that the Lord does not want complicated prayer, nor many reflections, etc; rather, he wants only a simple look of love. Then the Lord lifts me up to a prayer in which one only receives, one does not give. Although in truth, it encompasses all because the soul receives first and when it is entirely merged with God gives all that it has received.

"I am hungry and have an insatiable need for being with God. It seems as if I have not been with him many hours. Every time I leave his presence, it is as if I have not been there with him and am always anxious to start all over again."

In April 1917, Conchita's first grandchild was born.

"I am a grandmother. Blessed be God! I am setting Elisa on the right track in her new life of motherhood. I taught her how to bathe the baby and many other things... I love this little piece of heaven, this tiny creature that God sent us through fervent supplications. How easily my heart becomes attached, my Lord!"

One by one, each of the remaining children began to get married. In July 1919, Nacho married. Lupe married in May 1924 and since only Salvador lived with Conchita, she wrote, "I feel like a dry corncob with only one kernel left."

On November 4th, 1923, Archbishop Luis M. Martínez, who was at that time auxiliary Bishop of Morelia, agreed to become Conchita's spiritual director. This spiritual guidance lasted until Conchita's death and it was of transcendental importance to her, as it was also for Archbishop Martínez.

In a letter written to Archbishop Martínez on the tenth of that month, Conchita summarized the state of her spiritual life. Here are a few paragraphs:

Considering all of God's favors, I need to live only for him, but nothing of that sort is happening. I am overly fond of sweets. I have reduced my prayer time because I feel dizzy – perhaps because of old age. I deal only with my children, since people tire me out and I feel that I sin against them due to my lack of charity for them.

I've gone through six years of painful loneliness, as if my soul dwells in a desert. I am afraid that this silence and this estrangement from the Lord is the effect of my lukewarm attitude and my infidelities.

Before, I would do penance by sleeping on the floor, but now with bronchitis, I sleep on the bed. Clearly, at my age, I can't do what I did before, even though I want to. Or is it that I lack love?

I feel as if I'm vegetating. I want to fly, but I don't have wings. I feel suffocated and can't find a way out. It's like I am in a tunnel, in a deep well, in darkness. I am hardly able to see my spiritual director. I confess with whomever I can. I see Father Felix very little. That's how I live. If I had Jesus, nothing else would matter! But he's hiding; perhaps he's unhappy with me.

When I finally come to feel his presence, a torrent of tears seems to invade me. I fail to understand myself. I am sensitive and yet hard as a rock. I am appreciative, but I do not reciprocate. I want to be a saint, but I do nothing.

Due to God's grace, I don't have great shortcomings, but I do lack charity in conversations. I lack God's presence and an interior life. I write and don't act. I see the faults of others, but I don't correct mine.

Before, I suffered when people saw me as a saint. Now, it doesn't matter whether they see me as an angel or as a devil; it's all the same to me. Before, I couldn't have it any other way but to die as a Sister of the Cross in the Oasis. And now, it doesn't matter whether I die in a rubbish heap, on a throne, or at the Oasis, or in any other place. Is it exhaustion? Is it I?

Frequently when I pray, I am either very sleepy or very tearful and that's all. I try to come up with a practical way to attain self-control and humility, and nothing more.

What can I do, Lord? I am 62 years old and I feel an urgent need to become holy, to be shaken. Like the two disciples at Emmaus, I feel as though evening is upon me and my day is about to conclude.

Excuse me, Bishop, this letter is very long. Speak to me with complete frankness, for I will be very grateful to you and God will reward you for it.

Five days later, Archbishop Martínez answered Conchita's letter. I will transcribe its principal parts:

Dear Mrs. Concepción Cabrera de Armida:

Even though I have not read the small notebook that you lent me, through papers written for Father Poulain (about the mystical incarnation) which I have read, and through your letter, I have been able to come up with a rather clear idea concerning your soul, and I hasten to communicate the following, just in case it can help you.

It is true that what you need to do is to simplify yourself. And the source of unification for you should be the supreme grace received through the mystical incarnation, which is the wellspring of the rest of the graces and the fruitful fount of external works. Love Jesus with the tenderness of a mother; Jesus has asked you for a maternal love. Imitate the Virgin Mary.

Unite yourself to Jesus as a victim, drinking with him the chalice of perfect love that, as the Lord has explained to you, consists of enduring whatever God may want, however he may want it, and because he desires it. Pay close attention to the internal disposition of being a victim, which demands total purity, complete abandonment and an intimate union with Jesus, because he is the only Victim who is pleasing to the Father. The external and internal sufferings will vary depending on God's goodwill, but of most importance is your disposition, your total abandonment, and more than anything, an extremely tight union with Jesus.

I do not find the narrative about your miseries to be unusual – what else can we bring forth, since we are nothing. But do not be troubled over that, since God is pleased when the splendor of his graces stands out above the smallness of our miseries; and those tiny miseries, by contrast, glorify God as well.

That internal loneliness, that absence of Jesus that you experience, is not, as you say, a punishment for failing to respond to the graces of God. That emptiness and that hopelessness is a work of God, so that you can imitate the Holy Virgin Mary in her solitude, that painful and fruitful stage of her spiritual priesthood.

Continue with your way of life and your penances; all of this, of course, depending on your health and your particular circumstances.

Ten days later, Conchita answered with this letter:

I have spent a happy week, reading and meditating on your precious letter, which has moved me deeply. Blessed be God, because I feel understood! I want to fly through that door you have opened for me. I want to live the grace of the mystical incarnation. I want to believe in it, love it, appreciate it, recognize it and execute God's design, even if it may seem like madness to me. I know I still have a long way to go, but at least, I now have a point of departure.

In May of 1924, Conchita's youngest daughter, Lupita, got married: "The moment has arrived when she will no longer be mine. My heart aches, even though Carlos (her fiancé) is very good. This is the last night that she will sleep here. I cry in silence, making sure no one sees me."

After the wedding and the reception, Conchita wrote: "So much commotion! I need solitude. Lord, I am not needed by anyone, as you can see.... Moreover, I think I am a burden. I say this without passion, calmly, but it is true.

"God has permitted people to marginalize me and abandon me. I have no use for the pretenses they show me. But I am very gullible: When I see a small thread of love, I grab it and hold on to it, and...understandably so, it gets torn with the lightest blow.

"When has my heart felt satisfied being far from you, Lord? Blessed are you, for even though it is by force, you are leading me to look for nothing but you!

"Yes, my Lord, it's okay.... Put sorrows all around me, so that I will not attach myself to anything else. Make everything scream at me, 'Not you!' This shall always make it easier for me to search for only you. How good God is to me! But sometimes I cry on my pillow, in silence and in the dark."

It is interesting to note that between the years 1917 and 1925, Conchita had a great writing spurt. In addition to many of the notebooks that comprise her *Account of Conscience*, she wrote fourteen books, and of these, twelve have been published and two remain unpublished.

NINTH PERIOD
1925

At this point in our story, I believe that the school of spirituality born of Conchita's life has been clearly defined; it is the spirituality of Christ as Priest and Victim – in other words, the Spirituality of the Cross. Nonetheless, I am going to describe the last stages of the spiritual journey of the Venerable Concepción Cabrera de Armida, because they contain precious teachings and uplifting examples for us.

The year 1925 represented a change in the course of Conchita's spiritual life, thanks to the direction of Archbishop Martínez. It is worth pausing a bit to reflect on these events.

On July 1st, 1925, Conchita engaged in week-long spiritual exercises at the house of the Sisters of the Cross located on Mirto Street in Mexico City. Archbishop Martínez gave her certain written topics which he recommended for her meditation each day.

Here is a summary of some of the meditations that Conchita wrote in her *Account of Conscience:*

"The Father gazes on me constantly with an infinite love. God's gaze always enriches the creature. We look so as to search, but God looks so as to give.

"Through that gaze, the Father communicates his essence to the Divine Word, because his gaze is fruitful. As he looks at us, he makes us his children, he makes us participants of his nature, and all that he owns will become our inheritance.

"The Father has looked at me with favor and I should glorify and thank him. I should no longer be looking at myself and my lowliness and my miseries; but I should raise my eyes toward the Father's gaze and allow myself to be loved. I should live as Holy

Mary did, loving and praising him: 'My soul glorifies my Lord for he has set his eyes on his lowly servant.'

"As the Father looks at us, he transforms us into his image and likeness. I am like a poor mirror that God has desired to peer into. I should no longer be considering the poor worth of the mirror, but rather, be joyful that it is God's image that is in it.

"My soul is a poor canvas, but God has painted on it. I should no longer be constantly crying over the shabbiness of the cloth, looking always at the backside of the design. I am going to turn the frame over once and for all and see it in full sunlight, so that I can live with gratitude and with joyful praises like Mary: 'My spirit rejoices in God my Savior, for he has done great things for me; he who can do anything.'

"Oh Mother, be my model! Take away this habit of mine of always looking at myself, for this holds me back, and I can't go forward."

Archbishop Martínez later spoke with Conchita and offered her some advice:

"He ordered me to keep my gaze solely on God and on the gifts that he has given me; that I should let my soul fly without restraints. I should no longer think of my weaknesses and miseries, but rather about the mercy and love of God, and I should appreciate more the graces that he has bestowed on me."

Archbishop Martínez truly knew how to direct souls. In reality, all who have been baptized ought to live focused on God's great gifts and not on their own miseries. If they do give in to their own miseries, then they cannot give thanks, cannot love, cannot praise; they do not advance, for they live in a state of discouragement.

Is it not sufficient for us to be partakers of the divine nature, true children of God, future inheritors, temples of his Spirit, chosen people, a consecrated nation and a royal priesthood?

Isn't this enough so that, despite our miseries, we can live joyfully and full of gratitude?

What holds us back? Is it our sins? Don't we have faith in the great value of the blood of Christ, of which only one drop would be sufficient to wash away the sins of all humanity?

What happens is that we never succeed in believing in the love, mercy and generosity of God for us, and this more than anything else gets in the way of our spiritual progress.

"I will follow my director's advice," concluded Conchita. "Upon entering this retreat, my soul was like an old throw rug, full of dirt, which had been given a good shaking and had had the dust fall off, so that one could begin to see the design printed on it and the quality of its workmanship. It is Jesus' precious image and I wish and hope that it will take its full form and light, so it can be seen and adored."

Then Archbishop Martínez asked her to meditate upon how her relationship with the Holy Trinity should be. Conchita wrote:

"With the Father, unlimited trust: I will see him as my good Father. My will shall be his, as was that of Jesus. I shall praise him for everything. I will constantly offer him the Word Incarnate, for the salvation of the world.

"With the Son, maternal love: how many times he has asked me for it! I will love him as a favored child, beloved in preference to others, the only one so cared for. I will love him with an appropriate tenderness every step of his life: his infancy, his public life and his passion. I will always be with him.

"This life should be one filled with faith and hope; I will love the Holy Spirit with all the strength of my soul, even in dryness and solitude, in deserts and in moments of abandonment.

"You, Holy Spirit, make me faithful. Make my existence fruitful. Purify my will, for I cannot go to you without you."

The next day, Archbishop Martínez told Conchita to meditate upon the respect that she owed to herself. Conchita wrote her reflections:

"A person filled with God is like a consecrated host. Under the humble human appearance, there is preserved in that person a heavenly treasure. Just as a host is adored, not for its appearance as bread, but for who is hidden in it, similarly a soul filled with God should respect itself, not for its human wrappings, which are worthless, but for what is preserved in it.

"I should, therefore, give my soul its proper place and its place is the heavens. I should do nothing that will debase it, but treat it as one treats a consecrated host.

"Oh, my God! I feel so guilty, for I have treated my soul harshly and with heavy blows most of the time, but I am going to do what the Bishop asked me to do. I am going to treat my soul with more sweetness, because it contains God's image. My soul cost Christ his blood and it contains divine treasures. It is like a piece of straw which is nothing and is totally worthless by itself, but the divine breath lifts the straw up to heaven and its very lightness helps it to fly."

On her third day of spiritual exercises, Conchita wrote: "Amazing! The cloudiness has lifted and I feel the sun shining! Even at night, I wake up speaking to the Holy Trinity and I feel the touch of the Holy Spirit.

"Is it possible that my chains have been removed? I do not ask for a palpable love, although I would like it to be such, but I do ask to find the way.

"During these past eight years, from time to time, the Lord has made his presence known, only to once again vanish into the heavens, leaving me in a most painful solitude. With so many sorrows on this earth, and without him! Is this how I am to continue? May his will be done.

"But with these exercises, I've had a respite, like a breath of fresh air. I feel happy and committed, with his grace, to the Cross that has been my patrimony.

"I feel alive, as if having received a heavenly thrust, as if having been turned loose, set free to fly. What, is winter gone? Or does it mean that I am going to die? Whatever he wants, may he be blessed!"

The next day, she wrote: "I woke up happy one night, talking with Jesus and the Father. My soul was on fire. I was awakened like this many times; it had been quite a while since Jesus had favored me in this palpable way, with tears and all. I already know that this is not essential, but it helps me. The Lord put me into a state of contemplation; it was one of those times when, at a certain point, a soul stands still, and that point is God."

Upon finishing these exercises, Archbishop Martínez gave her his last instructions: "Simplify your spiritual life around the grace of the mystical incarnation. This is the most important thing for your progress. It is important that you do three hours of prayer every day. Regarding penances, do only those which are permitted by your age and health."

The first few days of August were very painful for Conchita; her daughter, Concha, the nun, became gravely ill.

But on August 7th, the Lord granted her a very special grace, which helps us understand that the levels of union with God, even here on earth, do not have a limit. Conchita called this grace, "invasion by God." She described it in a letter to Archbishop Martínez:

Yesterday, after several painful days, I experienced an exhausting invasion by God, something more than just touches and intervals of rest from the Holy Spirit. It was like a profound penetration of God's love that radiated not only throughout my soul, but into my body as well. Tears came to me. I couldn't hold back the tears anymore. I was on a bus, going to a Mass in honor of a lady who died, my doctor's wife. It was during the Mass that the experience was strongest. I felt a martyrdom of love, for a creature's nature cannot resist those avalanches of the infinite. God, God, God... that is what I felt and nothing more; but it was so much, it was everything, it was him. He absorbed me powerfully in his divine essence; it was like being lost inside him, because he wouldn't fit in me. What an experience. . . !

A few days later, Conchita had this other experience: "On many occasions, I sensed and saw the gaze of Jesus upon me. My heart still beats fervently just remembering it. What a gaze; so sweet; so tender; so penetrating; so loving! I like knowing that Jesus loves me and feeling his infinite love; yet when the moment comes, I can't take it and I want to be a gopher and hide."

During the following days, Conchita continued to feel the effects of these new "invasions by God."

"I desire to always be with him, even in the midst of the crowds and all my daily activities. He has lifted me up on high and he won't let go. I often offer the Father his Incarnate Word. He has conquered me and I have overcome various obstacles with a smile on my face. This invasion by God has saturated me, as though I am thoroughly absorbed in him, like milk in coffee, like sugar in water."

On August 16, she wrote: "My soul continues to be absorbed in God. And with him, I don't care about the sufferings, the rebuffs and the humiliations. Jesus calls me day and night. He steals my heart and I melt within him, my All! He wants me to stay with him, to speak about him, to do everything for him.

"My God! What is happening to me? Did I awaken? Did I revive? Where were you, Life of my soul? Will you leave me again?

Will I lose you once more? Whatever you desire! But meanwhile, I will enjoy you; I will beseech you; I will adore you, humbled beneath the weight of your love."

Because of her human nature, Conchita felt unworthy of such special favors from God. Sometimes she would experience a "spiritual shyness," which in reality was a resistance to God's action. Regarding this, Archbishop Martínez wrote to her:

You say you would rather endure a great penance than 'to undergo the shame' of being united with God and hearing his loving words. Very well, God is satisfied with your humility. But know that union with God is worth much more than many hours of penance, and that it is more pleasing to God to unite himself with a soul that offers no resistance than all the sacrifices that can be offered to him by that same soul. Understand that these unions are more meritorious and more fruitful for the Works of the Cross, for your spiritual sons and daughters and for the whole world, than anything else you can do for him. Of course, that God unites himself in this way with your soul is out of your hands, but you can and must receive these graces lovingly and use them generously for the benefit of the Church.

Conchita answered his letter:

I received your letter, for which I am grateful with all my soul.... I have experienced this kind of prayer; it transcends all time; it is like a total immersion in God, a complete union. But where will I end up if this continues? At an earlier time I would resist it, pretend it didn't happen, but since you have encouraged me to surrender my heart completely, I wonder if my miserable being can stand it? I have done it, but I have already told you how I am.

Archbishop Martínez responded:

> You should not resist this 'absorption by God,' unless you have something urgent to do. Is he not your Master? If he kills you with love, by what better hands to suffer it, so surrender yourself with abandon! Do not resist any further. This surrender without resistance is not in opposition to the spiritual shyness that springs from your humility.

At the end of August, Conchita became bedridden with a serious illness. Jesus reminded her that her sufferings, united with his, would gain graces for the salvation and sanctification of many spiritual children. For he had proclaimed her mother of many souls, especially those of the Works of the Cross. He promised her that she would be quite spiritually fruitful if she only embraced, with love, her daily crosses.

That grace of the "invasion of God" continued to produce great effects in Conchita:

"When I search for where my heart lies, I always find it with him or thinking about him.

"I have boldly turned myself over to Jesus, without fear, with incomparable tenderness, with great maternal love and unimaginable warmth.

"Now I feel I am rich, although poor. In the heights, although lowly. I am filled with the Word, although I am empty with my nothingness.

"I love Jesus, the Word, with the love of a mother: pure, generous, without selfishness, sacrificial, immense, holy, profound and disinterested in all other things. For this reason, I have died and now he lives in me.

"Now I experience the freedom of the children of God; I see new horizons of trust. This is a new dawn in my spiritual life."

On August 20th, Archbishop Martínez gave Conchita this advice in order to simplify her spiritual life:

"May your life consist solely of a gaze of gratitude and love and within this gaze, put all your abandonment, your petitions, and your intercessions for others.

"Do everything 'through him, with him and in him,' uniting your soul always with that of Jesus."

On October 20th, Conchita wrote: "I feel the real presence of God and his love, and I regret not having a heart as immense as the ocean to be able to return his love. I invoke the Holy Spirit and I offer my beloved Word to the Father with inconceivable tenderness and love. This is what Jesus has asked of me:

"Your task, my child, is to continually offer a mystical Mass. This, too, is the goal of the members of the Oasis: an offertory by which they offer themselves to the Father with me. It is a consecration by which they state along with me, 'This is my body, this is my blood.' Never cease doing this, offering me and offering yourselves with me for the sake of the Church and all humanity. Do this in memory of me."

On November 28th, Conchita wrote to Archbishop Martínez and described another very special grace: "On Thursday, the Lord suddenly granted me a sense of his presence that not only bathed my soul, but my body as well, as if impregnating it with something divine. How unusual! I remembered another occasion right after receiving Communion when a light flowed from inside me and passed through my body and Jesus said to me, 'This is the purification of matter.'

"This has brought me to a new regard for myself and my poor

body, which the Lord also loves and blesses. How amazing!

"Another grace I received this week was this: I found myself offering the Word without even thinking about it. It pleased me that without even thinking about it, I would do this. Even if I were in the middle of a crowd, I would feel the touch of the Holy Spirit, who would remind me, "How great is God's goodness!"

On December 3th, Conchita's daughter, who was in the convent of the Religious of the Cross in Mexico, became so ill she became delirious. The Mother Superior called Conchita and let her stay with her daughter as long as she wanted.

On the 11th, Conchita's daughter received the Anointing of the Sick. On the 12th, she became lucid and was able to receive Communion. Conchita wrote: "Finally, she recognized me and she called out to me, 'My beloved mommy!' Poor child, it tears my heart to see her suffer like this. I look upon her and I offer her to the Eternal Father, together with Jesus, telling him to take her, that his will be done. Oh, how much she suffers and I do, too! My God, blessed be God!"

On December 19th, this holy Religious died. She was Conchita's favorite child, especially since she had consecrated herself to God in the Oasis.

On the last day of the year, Conchita felt this loss very deeply. "With my heart torn to pieces, but with a resigned soul, loving, adoring and blessing the divine will of God, I came home to await a new year close to Jesus."

TENTH PERIOD

1926 - 1927

In these last chapters, it is not my intention to describe any more detailed facts concerning Conchita's life or spiritual journey. Rather, I have chosen certain passages from her journal which could be valuable for our own spiritual lives:

January 2nd: "God has suddenly given me an insight that has taught me that I should no longer think solely of myself, whether I am to suffer or not to suffer. I should forget about myself completely and offer my pain to Jesus, however great or small it may be, without even thinking about it. And I sense a tremendous grace that, wherever I may be, I am peaceful and happy, knowing that God's will is done. My tears are quite another matter."

January 16th: "I cannot pray; I try to, but nothing happens. I feel so far from Jesus. I try hard, but it is useless, so all I can do is curl up under his will. All I want is what he wants, nothing more."

January 20th: "I feel like a disoriented gopher; as if anesthetized by the Holy Spirit; in a kind of stupor, as though I am not myself. How can I feel so alone, if I have my God? Maybe it is because I have been so occupied with external things such as sewing, making bread, answering letters, etc. I feel this way even though I do everything through him, with him and in him. How much I have profited by this!"

January 28th: A passage from a letter from Archbishop Martínez: "The ultimate in holiness is adherence to the divine will, without condition or compromises, with great joy, with real passion. The greatest thing that Jesus did in this world was to adhere to the will of his Father with absolute perfection. Well, may you do the same. Be Jesus in all things, but especially in fulfilling and loving the will of

God."

January 29th: "My God, I feel that with your grace, my soul has taken flight. I experience more union with you. I also feel more love for my neighbor so I can easily return good for evil, forgiving with generosity. I also feel more detachment from things of the world and human affections."

January 30th: "I have felt joy even in the midst of pain. I am amazed by this. My suffering is so intense at times that it brings me to tears. And yet, there in the depths of my heart, I know not where exactly, I still feel joy because God's will is being done, even at the cost of my life. I am attracted to God's will; it thrills me, it absorbs me and it captivates me. I see his will as perfect goodness, even if it crucifies me."

February 3rd: From a letter from Archbishop Martínez: "This passion for the divine will which God has instilled in you is one of the greatest gifts that God can bestow on a person in this life. It is the essence of union with God; it is the center of holiness itself. It is the very depth of love. If you never had any other virtue or received any other grace from God but this one, it would be enough for you."

February 4th: "I cannot deny that I have taken a giant step in my process of adhering to the will of God. Blessed be God! I cannot take credit for this. I have suddenly come upon this pearl in my hands. This is Jesus in me. It is thus…

"And I have discovered that in fulfilling the will of God, therein lie all the virtues: patience, sacrifice, humility, generosity and love which embraces all things. Jesus asked me to simplify my life and now I know how to do this."

July 22nd: "Today I feel crushed, indifferent, in darkness, as if abandoned or forsaken. I am trying hard to have patience. I feel as if he who sees all, hears all and feels all is deaf to me."

August 13th: "What is happening to me? I feel such indifference and coldness, and yet at the same time, I talk about love and feel this maternal love that grows, expands and becomes immense. This happens without my knowing who stirs up this feeling in me, which flows like water from a dam that has burst, with a force that astounds me. What obstacle has broken loose from my soul that has caused this stifled volcano to erupt with such force? I feel a sensitive and captivating love that pierces all and divinizes all. In the past, I felt this maternal love for Jesus like burning embers. But now it is a blazing fire and it fills my entire being like perfumed incense.

"I don't think this sensation will last long, for I am familiar now with Jesus' ways. But let it be as he wills. I shall be like a mother who loves her son the same whether he is nearby or far away, whether he is visible in the light or obscured in the darkness."

August 16th: "I am ill. My temperature has come down (but my heart is on fire). I have many aches and pains and I am very exhausted. Blessed be God! This is all I want to say from now on. How much I love him!"

On August 18th they told Conchita that Chabela, her daughter-in-law, was in danger of dying. Something had gone wrong with her pregnancy. Conchita went to visit her and stayed to care for her however she could. They had to operate on Chabela. The baby was stillborn. The mother was seriously ill until October. Conchita was at her side constantly. This is how she describes those two months:

"I arrive very early in the morning at Chabela's house, to deal with doctors, medical treatments, visits, etc. I have no time for prayer. All I can do is tenderly caress Jesus. My soul has entered a journey of maternal love for him and for all people. There is no equal to maternal love: it is so resourceful, so bold, so holy and so authentic. It does not find any suffering too difficult; it just caresses, consoles and kisses. Maternal love is content seeking happiness for the child, even at the cost of great suffering.

"That is how I love you, the Love of my life. I love you with tenderness, with passion, with all my heart, with my life and a thousand more, if I had them."

On November 27th, Conchita's youngest daughter, Guadalupe (Lupe), became gravely ill. She, too, was pregnant and something was not right with the pregnancy. It was an emergency, and they rushed her to the British Hospital, where she was operated on. The baby survived for only five minutes. They barely had time to baptize the child. Conchita would spend her days by her daughter's side at the hospital. At night, she would go to Lupe's house to care for her granddaughter.

In her diary, she commented: "I would like to be like Mary (the sister of Lazarus who sat at Jesus' feet to listen to him), but instead, I live the life of Martha (the other sister who tended to the needs of the Lord). This is what YOU want, my Jesus, and so this is what I want also, although I long to be before the tabernacle."

December 10th: "Jesus is still making a "Martha" of me, especially with Chabela, who lives nearby. First I go to the British Hospital near Chapultepec. Then I go to Lupe's house in the Roma neighborhood. I have to take two trolleys and then walk the rest of the way. I am absolutely exhausted by the time I eat supper. I offer my stair climbing, which causes me so much pain – to the point of tears – to Jesus. I also offer my tiredness to him and his absences from my life. But I behave badly toward him. I arrive so very tired with aches and pains in my legs and feet, and therefore, I spend but a few moments with him, and then I have to lie down, and from my bed, I express my love to him. This little donkey cannot take much more. And Lupe still cannot get out of bed and yesterday her sitter left. I have sent Gertrude to take her place; and me, I do what I can around the house before leaving to care for them. Blessed be God!"

In the preceding paragraph, we see the balance that the great saints discover between the need to be in prayer and the demands of charitable work. Conchita was now sixty-four years old and she had plenty of aches and pains. She could have given plenty of reasons for freeing herself from so many obligations. But Jesus asked this of her, and she was faithful to her duties as mother, mother-in-law and grandmother.

January 4th, 1927: This is a passage from a letter from Archbishop Martínez:

Allow Jesus to live in you. Don't let your external duties impede his presence in you. You will achieve this allowing Jesus to take care of everything. Let him be the one to cure people, to entertain guests, to answer letters, etc. You are just to be his instrument, his disguise, his scribe, or better yet, his mother who carries him as a child in her arms and in her heart. It is for him to work; what you will do is carry him. How much will Jesus fill your words, your activities, your works, if you just let him work. Then these occupations will not be a distraction, but rather a new way of getting even closer to him.

January 20th: "Now I am occupied solely with greatly loving the three Divine Persons and asking them to love me. I let myself be filled with any One of them, whoever comes to me first. They each have the same attraction, beauty, goodness and love. As I approach any One of them, I breathe in the perfume of all Three because they are all one sole Divinity. Their unitary whole gives me such joy.

"Sometimes I remain fixed on God the Father, and I feel that infinite Majesty, that paternal love that draws me to him. On other occasions, the Holy Spirit comes to me, completely overpowering and impregnating me with his substance, which is to say, his love. At other times it is Jesus, the Love of my life, my joy and my hope, who comes to me and fills me with everything.

"I do not experience this all the time, or I would surely die. The experiences pass and I am again my usual self, and this really bothers me. But I remain saturated by that gentle breeze that brushed me leaving its dew."

February 22nd: "Quickly I quieted myself to love Jesus, and I felt an extraordinary and divine effect. Instead of feeling my love for him as always, I felt his love for me. I know he loves me, but to actually feel that love is very different from just knowing about it. In an instant, I felt an ocean of love in my heart. It drowned out all my sinfulness, all my human frailties. For a moment, I felt a total invasion of love. I felt the tenderness of that love, its intensity like fire, a sweetness that impregnated my entire being. I felt totally loved, my God! Surely, if the sea engulfs us, we remain lost inside of it.

"Our roles have changed. It is he who calls me, instead of my calling him. He searches for me, and not the other way around. He fills me, engulfing me in his gaze and his love. Now for sure, I must allow myself to be loved. I can't caress him, but rather let him caress me. I feel that all my loving feelings and caresses are coarse, rough and crude, compared with his infinite and sweet love. Oh, my God! What else can I say?"

March 12th: "When I talk to him, I just say, 'Yes, yes, love me so much. I let myself be loved by you, and this act is my way of loving you as never before, without any resistance and without self will.'

"I am invaded by something I do not know. Oh yes, I do know; it is he. It is he who has taken complete possession of me, of this dilapidated, ugly and dry ranch. But he is eternal spring and he beautifies this ranch, so that he can enjoy the beauty of his own creation. He has not spoken to me, but he is pouring himself into this immense void. Is this real? Of course it is; I feel it overflowing inside my chest. Yesterday, it hurt all day. In the past, thinking about the suffering of Jesus used to cause me to feel a lot of grief and compassion. But now when I think about it, I feel his pain, and thinking about him, I see him through the eyes of my soul. Oh, my Jesus, how good you are!

"Lately, his words penetrate my soul like light through the

darkness enlightening me; like water through the mire cleansing me; like heat through ice melting my coldness; like a soothing balm healing my spirit; like divine manna satisfying my hunger. Oh my Jesus! How awesome you are!"

June 22nd: Conchita had to leave for San Luis Potosí on urgent family business. They told her that her brother Octaviano was gravely ill and his wife was also sick. She rushed to help them and console them. She stayed there until July 13, caring for their needs until the emergency passed and her brother began the process of convalescence.

September 8th: Conchita went to Morelia to do her yearly spiritual exercises. This time she did them in the house where Archbishop Martínez was hiding because of the religious persecution that began in June of 1926. These persecutions were far crueler and more radical than those of 1914. Conchita's spiritual exercises were very fruitful and produced much spiritual growth for her.

September 10th: "All it took was to enter the chapel, for Jesus to come into my soul like an overflowing torrent, enlarging my heart so that it could be filled with his presence even more. He then told me, 'I want to give myself to many souls through you. I am going to fill you so you overflow and give of my essence to the whole world. Above all, my priests will share in this grace.'"

September 14th: "My Lord, they have told me that they may have to operate on me because of the illness I have inside me. I am scared. I really don't want to bother anyone, but I also want to forget my 'Self.' I throw myself blindly into your paternal arms and I beg you not to consider what I want or don't want. May your holy and wise will be done in my life.

"If I am at the point of death, I would like to be assisted by my spiritual director, or one of the Missionaries of the Holy Spirit, or maybe my son Manuel could come. But if you want me to leave this earth alone and abandoned by God and all humanity, with a great struggle or in peace, with pain or calmly, with my children or without them, here or there, by day or by night, bothering others or not, I only want your will to be done.

"My Mother, I cannot do anything by myself, but with you, as you take my hand – you who know my inconstancy and weaknesses – I can reach the end doing what Jesus asks of me, out of pure gratitude and love."

September 15th: Conchita got up early and went into the presence of the Lord to present the "burial of her 'Self.'" Later, she wrote this amusing obituary:

"Today, at 7:30 in the morning, the 'Self' of Concepción Cabrera de Armida passed on to a better place. Jesus and Mary ask for your participation in lifting her up in prayer so that she not rise from the dead and return to her old ways.

"I hope it happens this way, my God! May I truly die to self so as to live solely in you and through you."

September 17th: "The Lord told me today: 'Love me and cause others to love me. Extend your love to the entire Church. You have to give my Church many children and purchase the renewal and perfection of many with your tears.'"

On September 22nd, 1927, the Lord visibly appeared to Conchita in a supreme state of affliction. He just uttered these words like a sigh of great anguish: "Oh, dear Mother!"

All through the following day, the echo of this cry reverberated through Conchita's soul. Kneeling at the tabernacle, she exclaimed, "Here I am, my Lord! What do you want of me?"

This question was the beginning of a long dialogue with Jesus which lasted until January 1931. Conchita called this discourse *The Confidences*. The theme of this discussion was just one thing: priests. This is a complete theology of the meaning of the priesthood and its proper spirituality. It spoke about the only road to their sanctification: the transformation of the self into Christ, Priest and Victim. It presented a very clear vision of reality, without ignoring the sins and flaws of priests. In addition, the Lord gave Conchita a new mission to fulfill during the last stage of her life. This was to love all priests as spiritual sons and to obtain for them the graces they needed for their transformation into Christ, by means of prayer and sacrifice.

These *Confidences* were first published in Morelia in three volumes, under the title *To My Priests.* Archbishop Leopoldo Ruiz granted an imprimatur for this book, which was addressed solely to priests. The publishing house "La Editorial La Cruz" published the second and third editions.

October 24th: "Jesus never leaves me. His memory and his tenderness do not leave me. It is as if there were an unceasing electrical current flowing from him to me and from me to him.

"I have noted great progress in my soul and it consists in the fact that my trust has grown because of his love. My setbacks no longer bother me in that, thanks be to God, they are not grave sins. Rather they are just trash, dust, weaknesses, the soil of which I am made. Now I know clearly that when we lose our peace over our miseries, that it stems from our pride and lack of trust in God. Now whenever I fall, I humble myself and turn my gaze toward Jesus, as if to say, 'Look at who I am. But I know who you are.' Then I continue on my journey without any further hesitation and I continue to love him as if nothing had happened. I wonder sometimes if this is not the result of some lack of sensitivity, but then I reach the conclusion that it is not so. What is happening is that love abounds and love covers all things. I think that if my love for others, which is so meager, can accomplish this, how much more the immense love of God. He covers our defects and miseries and he consumes them in the fire of his love.

"This light has lifted a great weight from my shoulders. These human miseries no longer delay me on my journey. Instead of being ashamed, I give a kiss to Jesus and together we turn the page. I then notice that my doing so gives great joy to my Lord. I used to get very sad and depressed over my shortcomings, but now they serve as steps as I climb upward toward him, to thank him for how he overlooks my weaknesses, to confess my feebleness, to cling to him and to seek refuge in the goodness of his heart."

November 3rd: This is a passage taken from a letter from Archbishop Martínez:

How I rejoice in the grace God has granted you! So many souls falter when they encounter their own shortcomings, because they do not know themselves or know God well. Whoever knows himself or herself well will not be surprised at any sign of weakness, because that person knows he or she carries within an endless depth of misery. 'What does the oak tree produce but acorns?' Whoever knows God well also knows that God's love overlooks our human weaknesses and, even more, the abyss of our miseries attract the abyss of his mercy. Stay on this path. After each fall comes a kiss of love and you proceed onward as though nothing happened. You have no idea how much this pleases Jesus.

On December 8th, the wife of Conchita's son, Nacho, had a baby. Conchita went to assist her until the 22nd. She had to leave because they told her that the wife of her brother Octaviano was gravely ill. She immediately took the train to San Luis, but she arrived too late and her sister-in-law had already died. She stayed with her brother for fifteen days, because he was devastated by this event.

ELEVENTH PERIOD

1928 - 1931

In the last years of Conchita's life, we see the same pattern we have observed in the previous chapters. There were alternating periods of spiritual solitude and seeming abandonment by God, followed by periods of consolation and enlightening communication. But there was always great progress in holiness, which essentially is a union with God.

For now, so as not to be too repetitive, I will choose just a few instances that are most relevant.

In 1928, Conchita was ill quite often: "It is probably because of my age, the weight of 64 years on earth. The doctor wants me to eat more and he is constantly giving me tonics to drink. But I feel a profound sadness that will not leave me even when I try to sleep; moreover, I feel Jesus is hidden from me. All this pain I offer up for priests."

Conchita's brother, Primitivo, the Jesuit priest, also became sick. He had been hiding in Conchita's house ever since the religious persecutions intensified. Therefore, Conchita was both a patient and a nurse. Her grandson, Panchillo, then came down with scarlet fever. This disease is highly contagious, so in order for no one else to catch the disease, Conchita took care of him by herself.

June 30th: "I have felt a great tranquility in the midst of my pain, a great peace amid my suffering, and more abandonment to the divine will. If I should die now, if it is time for Jesus to take me home, so be it. I still have strings attached from my heart to this earth, but I shall sever them and sacrifice them because I just want to do his will."

From November 22nd to November 30th, Conchita practiced

her spiritual exercises with Archbishop Martínez in Morelia. Her final resolutions were these:

"To be Jesus, looking at the Father with Jesus' eyes and loving the Father as Jesus did, and like Jesus, having a passion for always fulfilling the Father's will in all things.

"To be Jesus for other souls, Jesus crucified and fount of life for many others.

"Lord, I offer myself for all priests, both living and dead, offering my sacrifices and prayers on their behalf. I offer to be Jesus Crucified for them."

1929: Conchita's soul was in a state of true desolation for practically the whole year. "When I approach the tabernacle, I feel cold, just like one more object there."

She was like this until November.

September 24th: Her son Salvador finally got married, the last one to do so. Conchita returned to her home before the reception dinner: "I couldn't go on. I feel like everything is over for me. I have retired ten beds, my husband's bed and one for each of my nine children. And now I am all alone. But I still have you, my Jesus, who never dies and who never leaves me. You will never abandon me.

"I will be a supplement of tenderness for my married children and I will rejoice in their happiness. Well, now you have me here alone, my Jesus; I am the servant of the Lord, let it be done to me according to your will."

On November 14th, Conchita went to Morelia to do her spiritual exercises for the year. She said that "she entered with fear and repugnance." Archbishop Martínez told her to make a complete and total commitment to the will of God. And so she did the following day:

November 15th: "I come to you ashamed, my Lord, to tell you that in the year since my last spiritual exercises, I have not fulfilled what I promised to do. Please forgive me.

"I have left pieces of my soul along the wayside and tears have poured daily from my eyes.

"I have lost you, my Jesus, and I come now to look for you because I cannot live without you. I know you are inside my heart, but you are so veiled, so hidden in the shadows, so deep in the iciness within, that I cannot see you. I am freezing to death in a coldness that I so want to change to fire, but I cannot do it...

"On these days that are solely devoted to you and being at your side, I want to make a renewed commitment to you of my entire being. If you should speak to me, I will be as equally happy as if you were to be quiet and hidden, leaving me in abandonment.

"I have been searching for light, but if you wish me to remain in darkness, then I will love that darkness, because that is what you want for me... I come to find the fount of living water, but if it is your wish that I die of thirst, then so be it, I will die of thirst... I came, my Jesus, to seek warmth from you, my Divine Sun. I seek love! But if it pleases you that I remain frozen like ice, then I want that, too, because that is your divine will.

"Am I making myself clear, my Jesus? I truly want to commit to these exercises. See how alone I am without you, but if that is what you want, then I want the same."

The most important thing to come out of these exercises was that the Lord broke the silence he kept with the servant of God for so many months, so that he could continue to explain her priestly mission for his Church. From then until January 1931, except for a few brief periods of silence, he kept on revealing to Conchita the *Confidences* that we have mentioned before.

Perhaps you are wondering in what manner Jesus communicated with Conchita. She explained it this way: "Sometimes I don't want to hear and I hear; I don't want to understand and I do understand; I don't even want to turn to face the Lord so as not to get involved, and still he encounters me and reprimands me.

"Sometimes he dictates to me more or less in words or phrases. At other times, it is not so. In an instant, he impresses within me a torrent of ideas. Sometimes he is very laconic, and yet, he leaves me with a clear understanding of what he wants me to understand.

"As a signal from God, without any intent on my part, my senses are suddenly dulled, as well as my memory and imagination. I remain like a blank paper, empty of self and void of my own composition of thoughts and ideas. He impresses within me a stream of perfectly formed concepts or phrases, even paragraphs that I understand in an instant.

"I interrupt this internal locution with questions or affectionate reactions and then the dialogue begins, because the Lord deems it important to explain these things to me.

"I don't hear his voice with my bodily ears, except on rare occasions. Sometimes I begin to doubt; I wonder if I am inventing these things and I am fooling myself. But I find myself with such peace that I am sure these things come from God. Furthermore, it is clear that if the Lord does not inspire me, I can spend hours in prayer and not come up with a single sentence. None of this is my invention; I could not come up with this, even if I tried.

"Sometimes, months go by and I hear nothing from the Lord. And at other times, I do not even have time to write down all that he tells me.

"Another way in which the Lord communicates with me is through my writings. I hear his voice that tells me: 'Write this down.' At the beginning I would hesitate, but in time I began to obey, and the moment I would grab the pencil, the Lord would begin to dictate to me, page after page of thoughts, sometimes things so lofty I couldn't possibly have invented them myself."

April 30th, 1930: "This is Holy Week and I wanted to be on fire for him, but instead, I was lukewarm. There was only one thing that happened to me. I felt myself to be, oh, my God, really a mother to him! On Good Friday, I felt Jesus' sufferings as though they were actually my own, and I truly wanted them to be mine; I wanted to yank Jesus from his persecutors and envelop him in my love.

"That Saturday, I went to see the movie "King of Kings," so as to reflect more on Our Lord's passion, on the love of my life. The movie had a great impact on me, but afterward, I just returned to my habitual coolness. Oh Jesus, have mercy on me!"

May 3rd: "This was a day of many memories. It has been 35 years since the first Cross of the Apostolate was erected on the 'Hacienda de Jesus Maria'. And it has now been 33 years since we founded the Religious of the Cross... During these years, so much joy, so much sorrow... so many deaths, so many tombs... so many vocations and countless graces...

"Already these Works have taken on their own identity and their priestly direction. How faithful God is in his promises!"

May 17th: "While I was having breakfast I felt as if a great light had been ignited in me. Jesus began to talk to me about the fruitfulness that exists in the interior of the Holy Trinity."

November 19th: "Oh my Jesus, truly your words are powerful and effective. You should see how much I feel your priests have become like my very own, how much I love them, how I forgive their shortcomings and have compassion for them. They are well centered in the depths of my heart and there grows within my soul a pure, holy and unselfish love for them. I want to do penance and sacrifices for each and every one of them."

December 9th: Conchita went to Morelia to do her spiritual exercises with Archbishop Martínez. She went there worried about the economic situation of her children. She did her exercises from the 11th to the 24th. On the 18th, she wrote the following:

"Lord, I turn myself over to you, truly and completely. If you want my children to fail in their businesses as I helplessly watch them suffer, let it be as you wish. If they need to leave and go far away to pursue their business enterprises, then I offer you this pain. If it be your will that I be left alone, that I die far from all that I love, so be it, I want your will to be mine. If you want, my Jesus – and I have already thought about this – that I live in someone else's home, without my oratory, without you in the tabernacle... Life of my life, I renounce everything for the sake of your love, loving your beloved will.

"As you can see, I no longer have a house; they sold it. I no longer have the Oasis. And even though I have you within my soul, you are so veiled that I cannot see you, I cannot hear you, and I cannot feel you. What can I do then? With a triumphant love, with all the holy enthusiasm of which I am capable, I will make your will be my will.

"I want to cleanse my soul of all its selfish desires in the fire of all these sufferings so I can offer myself to the Father, uniting myself to you on behalf of all priests. Amen."

December 21st: "Suddenly I felt something like electricity inside and out, with a desire to ignite a fire, the dynamite of divine love in all of humanity. I would like the whole world to be one great Mass, one sole sacrifice, one sole Jesus, in whom we would all be absorbed. And I desired this, above all, for Jesus' pastors, the priests. 'Do you agree, my Jesus?'

And the Lord answered me:

"'I told you that you would ignite the hearts of many. My reward to you for having surrendered yourself to me shall be to envelop you in a fire that will spark the hearts of many souls.

"'This fire is the Holy Spirit. He will not always be as perceptible as he is for you now, but he will always be in you, for the good of innumerable souls.'"

December 24th: "I feel this great prompting from heaven to give God to others and to envelop thousands of souls in the presence of God. I feel like a lioness defending her cubs against an enemy, at all costs. I feel this way about everyone, but especially the priests. The zeal of a warrior has been inflamed within my soul, like some combustible fuel ready to ignite. My heart is fervent with a desire to give my God holy priests; priests filled with fire and transformed, as he explained to me, in the unity of the Holy Trinity. I am not satisfied with merely attaining my own salvation, but rather, I long to share Jesus with others. Why, my God? What is happening to me?

"And my Lord responded: 'Because this is your mission.'"

During this time, Conchita once again insisted to her spiritual advisor that she be made one of the Religious of the Cross. Her greatest desire was to live the rest of her life in a convent, completely dedicated to a life of prayer. When her last child was married, she saw her way clear to this goal that she had desired for so long. But Archbishop Martínez was very concerned about Conchita's age; he told her that this was not advisable and she should no longer think about this. On December 28th, Conchita wrote:

"My beloved Jesus, today I offer to you perhaps the greatest sacrifice of my life, because I have put to death the greatest desire of my entire life. Why should I tell you what you have seen in the depths of my being, year after year. Today, out of love for you and because it is your will, I renounce the deepest dream of my life. Receive my sacrifice on behalf of your priests.

"Goodbye, my beloved Oasis! I shall leave to struggle and live outside of this center of my life. No, No! The center of my life is the will of God and I shall live in this center for the rest of my life.

"And what does Jesus tell me:

"'Thank you, my child. I want you without self-will, even in the most legitimate and holy matters. See, today you have entered deeper into the depths of my heart, and I into yours.'"

1931. In January and February, the Lord spoke once again to Conchita regarding her mission with respect to priests: she must pray for them, sacrifice herself for them and obtain graces for them through a hidden life of true holiness.

On March 25th, the Religious of the Cross celebrated the 25th anniversary of the main grace bestowed upon Conchita, the mystical incarnation. They invited Archbishop Leopoldo Ruiz and the Missionaries of the Holy Spirit to this celebration. Conchita did not want to attend. However, in obedience to her spiritual director, she did attend the Mass and the breakfast that followed. Later, she wrote in her diary:

"I would like to be a little mouse and just hide in some hole where no one could see me, and there, in solitude, offer my thanks to the Father, to Jesus, and to the Holy Spirit for so many favors that have come from that great grace bestowed on me 25 years ago. But it didn't work that way. Jesus wanted my life to be public for the sake of others... If that is what you want, Lord, then that is what I want."

From April on, Jesus spoke no more to Conchita until five months later. This was a period of great desolation for her spirit.

On the 8th, 9th, and 10th of September the Lord resumed talking to her regarding the intimate nature of the life of the Holy Trinity. Regarding this, Conchita commented:

"What the Lord told me has left me in a state of envelopment in God. Ever since that day, I have felt filled by something divine. This time, this feeling has lasted quite a while. It drives me to interior recollection; it lifts me from the earth and it immerses me in God.

"I feel a special delight in knowing that God is so happy within the intimate life of the Trinity, in that eternal and infinitely fruitful relationship amongst the Father, the Son and the Holy Spirit. It is this ever renewed love, so unselfish, that delights over the infinite joy of God."

September 26th: Conchita experienced another "invasion by

God":

"This invasion has seized me and it won't let go. It enlivens me even when I'm in the midst of a crowd, as I'm walking down the street, or doing my daily chores, and I feel that I am penetrating deeply into God.

"My soul moves through the humanity of Jesus and from there is taken to the Divinity of the Word. I no longer remain in Jesus as man, but rather as God, and then he leads my soul to the unfathomable depths of the Trinity. Each of the Divine Persons seems so perceptible that, if I didn't know they were three distinct Persons, I would contemplate each one with great clarity, distinguishing each by the effects each has on my soul, though based on the principle of unity."

October 14th: "I feel as if my soul were a sponge, and if one would squeeze it, out would pour God. What a terrible way to explain my feelings! Now you know how foolish I am. But really, these are things that are impossible to explain."

November 11th: "Throughout my life, I have experienced three kinds of love for God. First, there is a humble love, yet at the same time a passionate love, filled with fervor and heavenly power, which only he can grant. Then I have felt that Jesus doesn't just want me to love him, but rather, that I let myself be loved, that I surrender without reservation to his love.

"And then, finally, I have discovered another love, humble yet bold. This love is childlike, trusting without limits. This love drives a soul to shut its eyes so as not to see what it is and then, clothing itself with gifts of God, it reaches for the Loved One with tranquility and naturalness. This "third love" consists not just in allowing oneself to be loved, but to desire and ask to be loved, to say to Jesus passionately from the depths of one's soul: 'Jesus love me, kiss me, caress me; no longer is it what I give to you, but what you give to me.'

"Lord, have mercy on me, but at the same time, love me

deeply; for only your love can satisfy my heart! Kiss me, embrace me, bind my heart to yours and my life with yours. It startles me to be so bold, but this is what Jesus wants now."

December 18th: "The Lord has explained to me the qualities of this 'third love.' It should be like the love of a child: simple, pure, innocent, unselfish and trusting.

"'But Lord, how can I love this way, when I am now seventy years old?'

"'Haven't I told you that the soul has no age?'"

December 26th: Conchita began her spiritual exercises for that year. On the fourth day of her exercises, she wrote: "Early in the morning, the Lord came to me like an inundation of fire, like a divine kiss, pure and holy...something inexplicable.

"The Lord told me: 'What you call kisses and caresses from God is a type of union of the highest and most intimate level. Oh, my daughter, love me and let yourself be loved!'"

The ancient mystics used this same language in the *Song of Songs* when they said: "Let him kiss me with kisses of his mouth! More delightful is your love than wine! Your name spoken is a spreading perfume" (Cant 1:2).

The masters of theology teach that the more a believer advances in the ways of spiritual union, the more the soul adopts a stance of passiveness before the powerful action of God, which surpasses and exceeds human capability, in such a way that the soul can only receive, and be grateful, and draw joy, in the love that God reveals.

Conchita concluded these days of spiritual exercises with the following brief prayer: "Uniting myself with Mary, I offer you my heart once more, so that it can love You with the tenderness of a mother and simplicity of a child, and with all the ardor and passion of this 'third love.'"

"Becoming like a child" before God is one of the necessary conditions for entering the kingdom of heaven (cf. Mt 18:3).

I would like to end this chapter by narrating an anecdote that occurred precisely during this period in Conchita's life.

The Reverend Mother Catalina García tells us that Conchita used to like sweets very much. For this reason, the Religious of the Cross would offer her two choices of dessert whenever she would come to dine with them.

It happened that on one occasion Conchita went to stay with the Sisters for a whole week, so as to carry out her spiritual exercises. It was Reverend Mother Catalina's turn to serve Conchita her meal during the last day of her stay. When she took her two desserts, Conchita told her:

"You know what, Catalina... it is really hard to choose which one I want, and so I will eat a little from each. On Monday, I ate my dessert with remorsefulness, on Tuesday with resignation, on Wednesday with tranquility, and on Thursday, with joy...."

TWELFTH PERIOD

1932 - 1937

1932: February 3rd: "Everything – except having suffered for God – passes without leaving us anything."

Conchita spent all of this year more or less as she did the previous ones: sick and frail, but caring for her own family with untiring dedication. Two more grandchildren were born and she continuously went from the hospitals to the homes of her daughters-in-law to be of service and care for the children.

All of this year, a dry period prevailed over her soul, in the apparent absence of Jesus.

September 10th: "The Lord told me: 'The remedy for the evils that have befallen the Church of Mexico and the entire world lies with the priests becoming transformed into me. So that I might work through them not only during Mass, but in all of their actions.

"When my priests, transformed into me, call out to the Father, the Father will hear them, because the prayer of his Son is infallible. I want to return to the world to save it, but in my priests. I must be in them."

October 24th: "Today, I tasted the sweetness of heaven. In a dream, or I don't know how, I saw Archbishop Ibarra; in an instant, I was immersed in an eternity of light and joy that made me understand the eternity of the blessed ones. It is the joy of the beauty and the delights of God himself. I felt God in a limitless point; I felt his Divinity absorbing my soul and everything that exists in a single point that is his unity. I felt the divine perfections in a single Perfection and I understood that all eternity is found in that point without time or limits. I understood mysteries and centuries and attributes and beauty and heavenly things, such that there are no words to explain them, because they are experienced without totally embracing their comprehension. Oh, my Jesus, blessed are you!"

December 10th: "This year has been generally dry, arid, full of thorns and illness."

1933: On March 6th, she began her week of spiritual exercises under the expert direction of Archbishop Martínez. The general theme was: How the soul must look for rest in Jesus, in his love, in his light, in his promises and in his peace. In these exercises, Conchita received new insights into the Divinity of Jesus Christ:

March 9th: "You should see, my Jesus, how the veils of my understanding that hide your Divinity have been drawn back....With divine light, I go beyond your human nature, and my soul is launched like a burning arrow to contemplate in you the divine, the eternal, the infinite, and my soul is brought to the unity of the Trinity."

March 10th: "Jesus told me: 'My body is like a step so that all might come to my Divinity. But the majority of souls are detained in my humanity, without continuing on to a relationship with the Word that is in me, inseparable from the Father and the Holy Spirit.'"

March 17th: "I write what I can. But I cannot transfer to paper what I understand in these depths of light. Who can explain what God is? How great, how infinite, how holy is God!... And to become man...! How can we not die out of gratitude and love!"

March 25th: "Feast of the Annunciation. I finished my exercises and later went to visit Our Lady of Patzcuaro. I enjoyed it very much. The entire way, divinity filled my soul. In every plant, in every cloud, in everything, I encountered the vestiges of his love."

May 2nd: "In the depths of my soul I feel an unshakable peace. I feel God in a more intimate and more perfect way. I feel him infinite...

"Upon kissing the crucifix, respect for the Divinity of Jesus comes to me and I love him in a new way, but without losing trust or tenderness. If I look at him as a Child, I see his Divinity; and if I contemplate him in the host or crucified, the same thing. I think of him at any age and there is God, with a new clarity."

May 22nd: "Just hearing the name of Jesus, or of the Father, or of the Holy Spirit, my heart trembles with excitement. By just remembering one of the three Divine Persons, I feel that the Divinity absorbs me, captivates me and introduces me to an intimate and profound silence, which unifies in me what is scattered and takes me to the depths of the unity of God.

"How ugly the earth seems to me! How empty the conversations! How cold the human hearts! How sad is the world compared with heaven!"

At the beginning of September, Conchita began to write another book, entitled *What Jesus Is Like.* On the 23rd of this month, she experienced great pain with the death of her favorite brother, Octaviano, who had helped so much with the Works of the Cross.

She spent the whole month of October writing her new book. She did not even write in her *Account of Conscience.* In December, it was done. Conchita wrote: "I hope that knowing how Jesus really is will produce great love for him in souls. Upon writing this little book, I felt that his presence was enlivened in me and that the third love was increased in my soul."

1934: From February until July of the year 1934, Conchita was very sick with a heart ailment and high blood pressure. And she once again suffered the "dark night of the soul."

By July 27th, she felt sufficiently well to go to Morelia for her spiritual exercises, which she so desired. The following day, she wrote: "What shall I do to break this dike which impedes me from seeing Jesus? I feel as if a thick, black cloud keeps me from seeing him and as if an infernal noise prevents me from hearing him."

Perhaps the reader is asking how the mystics are able to pass through such contradictory states of the soul. How is it that, since they experienced such a great union with God, this experience seems to be canceled, to give way to loneliness and abandonment?

What happens is that our consciousness is so occupied by what we are experiencing in the present that all previous experience is displaced. For example, if you are dying of hunger and thirst, having been satiated on other occasions will not be of help to you.

Besides, we are absolutely inept regarding the things of God, so that when the Lord does not grant us enlightenment, we feel lost.

However, God never abandons his children. On the contrary, in the midst of these trials he sustains in them the infused virtues of faith, hope and love, which are not experienced in the realm of the senses, but only in the highest pinnacle of the spirit.

July 29th: "'Jesus, I have already given you everything. How can I increase my gift?'

"'You can return to me my very self, which I have given you, accepting the absence of my perceivable presence, making this sacrifice for the salvation of many, and especially for my priests.'"

During these days of retreat, Archbishop Martínez reminded Conchita that the Lord had asked her to imitate Mary in her years of solitude, when she accepted remaining on earth without her Jesus, for the good of the Church.

August 16th: "Today I feel a new type of love – a wordless union with Jesus, a union of wills, a communication of feelings, a union of all loves that have been made into one single love. What is this, my Jesus?

"'It is love in its perfect simplicity, that which brings all the parts together in a single entity: the Divinity.'"

December 16th: "I prepared the Posada and the Nativity for my grandchildren so that they would remember the Christ Child.

"I feel tired. I have had so much sadness in my heart these days and so many deceptions on earth. Blessed be God!"

February 1935: "The consolation and words of my Jesus have been lost to me. I gave them back to him. I offered them for the sake of priests, as he had asked of me. But this is so hard!"

June 10th: "All that is good requires so much effort! The penances, the prayer...I know that I love Jesus by faith and by tangible flashes of grace. But I, once again, remain in a harsh and tedious desolation."

July 12th: In a letter to Archbishop Martínez:

> I hardly understand what I read and what I pray. I fear that I have fallen into a lukewarm state. But I think that it is not so, because if it were, my present state of emptiness and impotence toward prayer would not be as painful as it is.

> You can't imagine how people tire me. How empty I find conversations and how superficial their opinions! People take joy in a silly outfit, or in a bit of praise, and do not think about God! I suffer from all this vanity and it makes me want to cry. So much emptiness in God's creatures and what disenchantment in human affection...! And Jesus, hidden....

August 16th: "I feel that I am now no more than a little firewood to burn in honor of Jesus. Even though I am not worth much, I believe that it is my duty to consume this body of clay, this will of mine, and all of me, as a holocaust for the benefit of others. I want to forget myself, whether it gives me pain or not, or whether it will harm me or not. My heart feels joy in thinking that in this way I am following Jesus, even though it may be from very far away. I feel that I am his in body and soul."

August 20th, in a letter to Archbishop Martínez:

What I am going to say may seem ugly, but it is necessary to be perfectly clear and honest with you. I hesitate to say it, but the truth is that the virtues have grown in me. They were weak and now they have begun to reign in my soul. My spirit only reaches out to heaven, to the divine, to the holy, to Jesus, to Mary. I feel a detachment from the earth, from all its creatures, without ceasing to love them. All of this is Jesus, who smiles upon me in the darkness; it is the Holy Spirit that is nudging me; it is the beloved Father that gives me his Jesus! Blessed be God!

September 10th, in a letter to Archbishop Martínez:

I hunger for love. I want my whole existence to be summarized as an act of continuous love. My soul is full of pain and love. Oh, how much my love for Jesus has grown through pain! I feel blessed by his Cross. I want to identify myself with him. I want his wounds on me, his blood, his sacrifice, his very heart.

How much I love you, Jesus of my soul! Because you are my Everything, because I am greatly indebted to you, and because you are mine. My soul is now delirious in its desire to possess you completely.

November 29th: "Traveling toward León (Guanajuato), Jesus invaded my soul. He definitely likes to travel. He has let himself be felt vividly many times on trains and has communicated with me."

January 10th, 1936: "What pains and satisfactions will the year that begins today bring me? New lives? Deaths? Joys? Sorrows? Whatever you wish, my Jesus!"

From this month of January until the day of her death (March 3, 1937), the Lord prepared Conchita for her exit from this world with a long period of spiritual dryness and physical ailments. It was her ascent to Calvary and it was her Crucifixion, prior to her final entrance into the glory of Christ.

From January on, Conchita did not hear the voice of the Lord again. Interior solitude was her faithful companion until the moment of her death.

In her *Account of Conscience*, on a page written on October 3rd, upon beginning her final spiritual exercises, she summarized the state of her soul during this entire year:

"I have cried a lot and I have suffered a lot with the absence of Jesus. But, thanks to God, I am abandoned in his arms and I am accepting these bitter trials as he wishes it, for the good of priests and the entire world. He asked me to give up hearing his words and receiving all tangible consolation, and I honored this request with my full knowledge and consent. What can be denied to the one you love?

"But it has not been the least bit easy. I have stumbled in the darkness and Satan wants me to believe that my life has been pure illusion and a total failure. But my faith, although weak, has sustained me, hoping against all hope and loving blindly, at times with an indifference more painful than the pain itself.

"I see my life as something that happened...as a faint memory, like an unconscious delusion. And I am in an endless solitude with no relief in sight, without even knowing if I love or not, if I have a heart or do not have one.

"I feel indifference even toward the tabernacle, toward Jesus, toward heaven...What emptiness, my God; how deep and how profound!

"But I only want what Jesus wants, even if my soul agonizes. I feel very honored that my poor merits may save or console a priest.

"I only wish to reassure myself that I am not responsible for the state in which I find myself. It is tremendously painful to have God and not to perceive him. But...isn't my road that of pain?

"Sorrowful Mother, Mother of the hopeless, help me and may everything be for the glory of the Father."

In her last exercises, Archbishop Martínez wanted Conchita to center her meditations around this theme: "The secret of perfect joy." And he explained to her how perfect joy is found each time that we lovingly embrace the Cross of Christ.

October 5th, in a letter to Archbishop Martínez:

Dear Father, I have read your meditation many times and I am intrigued by your ideas, but in all sincerity I cannot understand that PERFECT JOY of which you speak, because my soul is in a thick fog: I believe, I hope and I love, but as if stuck in a never-ending tunnel in which my sobs are lost. Where is Jesus? What has happened to him? Where has he possibly hidden that I cannot find him.

You tell me that now my union with him is closer on this Cross, but...why, my Jesus, being so close, does it seem that you do not hear me? Why do you disappear when my soul wants to embrace you? Why is this emptiness so harrowing, if you are filling it? What has happened to my spiritual life, in which I always found you?

I already know the why of all of this, but let me cry at your gates accepting this darkness, this "senselessness of your cross," this madness of my life...

What can I do to make the best of these exercises that undoubtedly will be the last ones of my life? I will weep close to your heart, asking to find perfect joy...

Most Sorrowful Mother, whom I love so much, show me how to suffer as you suffered, and to love Jesus as you loved him in your terrible solitude.

October 13th, in a letter from Archbishop Martínez:

The joy of the one who loves is not bound to the voice or visible charms of the Beloved. Joy springs from the security of his love, the certainty of his presence, and the unbreakable nature of this union. Although the Beloved is silent, although sleeping, although hidden, nothing can impede the triumphant joy of whoever carries him in the intimate recesses of the soul, without anything or anyone ever being able to snatch him away.

In a mysterious manner, the little light of faith, which no darkness can extinguish, shows the soul, the presence of the Beloved, and makes it see that he lives within the soul in a very close and perfect union.

Finally, on October 14th, the Lord deigned to console his daughter, saying to her only these words: "Do you believe that I am heartless? Do you believe that I am not moved by your pain? But allow me to work. You do not know how much glory my Father has received with your patience and how much benefit many priestly souls have received, thanks to your martyrdom."

Conchita commented:

"These words made my soul quiver. They were a soothing balm, because his words work with power and they infused me with courage so that I could continue on without him in regard to his perceivable presence, and live in the martyrdom of his absence. I will not complain anymore. I will let him work freely in my soul, taking pleasure in his will. Now I do understand the meaning of perfect joy."

October 19th, in a letter to Archbishop Martínez:

> Today one thing has caught my attention: a very deep peace, a contentment, a serenity, a...JOY. Despite the current state of my body and my soul... Despite the bitterness of my martyrdom... I feel a sweetness in fulfilling the will of Jesus. Despite the pain of his silence, I feel joy in pleasing him. Despite the distress of lacking his solace, I feel patience and generosity in my surrender. Can these be the seeds of perfect joy?

October 21st: "Internal suffering has martyred my heart today, but only on the surface; in its interior, a holy joy, a divine happiness, has not ceased."

October 24th: "I have had a very painful day. I have not been able to find comfort or a restful place for either the body or the soul; but I have peace in my heart and I take delight in what pleases Jesus, because my suffering gives more spiritual life to the Works of the Cross for the glory of the Father. Am I not to take pleasure in all that pleases my Lord?"

October 31st: "I never imagined all the riches that PERFECT JOY encompasses. I have felt that this ought to be the ultimate ideal for those who belong to the Works of the Cross."

November 29th: "I continue to spend most of my time in bed, with much pain, offering everything to my Jesus for priests. Jesus hidden...all that is left is a memory of him, like an illusion that has passed, like a passion and a delirium that have now been extinguished and this brings me to tears. But I have peace and joy in abandoning myself to the sweet and holy will of God."

December 8th: This is the last paragraph in her *Account of Conscience*. From this day on, Conchita did not write anything except for a few letters to Archbishop Martínez. On this day, she celebrated her 74th birthday and, at this point in her life, she would have a little less than three months to live.

"Jesus, silent...in spite of how much I asked him to give me my gift today. I spent this beautiful day of Mary Immaculate, in bed, sick and with sorrow in my soul, but in peace, offering everything for priests. I have received many Masses as gifts... from my son Manuel, 30...Oh my Jesus, blessed are you, and all for your glory!"

This was the last entry that Conchita wrote in her diary.

HER DEATH

January 29th, in a letter to Archbishop Martínez:

If you could see how my soul needs warmth, courage, Jesus. What shall I do? I already know that I should put your holy advice into practice: To ponder that Jesus loves me and that I love him. The only thing that I do is rest my tired head against his heart and cry upon seeing my spiritual life as undone. And that is how I spend my nights and days.

I have become a disaster and I refuse to believe that this will be my way to heaven. My life is reduced to this: I get dressed and then go to my armchair, with no ability to get around. I never thought that I would finish in this state of inertia, in physical and moral exhaustion. Well...why bore you. And now, I cannot even write.

February 15th, in a letter to Archbishop Martínez:

My state of health continues to deteriorate. We will see if I die from this. Whatever God wills.

And alone, alone...having him just a step away. The light from the lamp in the tabernacle enters under the door and I do not even have the strength to go see him, because I am unable to stand. Day and night I am in the armchair, sometimes crying because of his absence, other times with a glacial indifference. Let's see what God wants...I am too tired to go on.

February 18th: Conchita wrote her last letter. It was addressed to Archbishop Martínez. It very briefly informed him of her health and ended with these words: "him...not even his shadow...."

On February 21st, the doctor gave up hope of saving her. The Religious of the Cross took turns caring for her throughout the night. On March 1st, she endured a very bad night. Mother Catalina García was watching over her, and Conchita, in the middle of great distress, said: "Oh, my dear Mother! It is as if Jesus and I had never known each other...."

During the afternoon of March 2nd, Conchita told the Religious of the Cross that attended her, to tell their sisters that she was very grateful to all of them and that they should become saints.

Close to midnight, her face acquired a deathly pallor and an expression of the deepest suffering. Archbishop Martínez whispered to her, "Conchita, although you may not feel him, Jesus is in your heart, loving you now more than ever...Offer yourself once more as a victim in union with Jesus...Offer your life for your children, for the Church, for priests...." Conchita opened her eyes and signaled agreement with just her gaze.

Approaching her agony, Conchita began to move from one side of the bed to the other, but without saying a word. When she became still, they checked her pulse and did not find one. A little while later, without even uttering one complaint, she slightly reclined her head and died. It was twenty minutes past midnight on March 2nd, 1937.

Father Guadalupe Treviño, who was present, gave us this testimony: "Those saints whom God chooses for the purpose of expiation end their lives drowned in a sea of sorrow. Thus was the death of Conchita.

"There are two things that I will never forget: her silence and her countenance. Her silence was like that august silence of Christ on the Cross. The supreme expression of pain is always silence, because it is so deep that it cannot even be shared.

"And her face...How do I express the bitterness and abandonment that I saw on her face? They were no longer her own features: They were of the face of Christ agonizing on the Cross...!

"It wasn't until she expired that her own appearance returned, but reflecting a peace which was contagious to all of us; it was almost an expression of joy.

"As he left the bedroom, Archbishop Martínez whispered to me: 'How I would like to be present right now at the fiesta with which they are receiving her in heaven...!'"

I have wanted to tell Conchita Cabrera's story from beginning to end, because there is no doubt that through the life and death of this admirable woman, God wanted to leave us a perfect model of what the Spirituality of the Cross is in concrete, daily living. And what was the essence of this holy life? "TO FOLLOW JESUS AS PRIEST AND VICTIM."

AS PRIEST, because the center of Conchita's spiritual life was to give glory to the Father, by offering Jesus to his Father as the only perfect and pleasing sacrifice in his eyes. We will see this clearly a little later, when we study the Chain of Love.

AS VICTIM, because Conchita lived and died offering herself to the Father in union with Jesus, through total and continual acceptance of his holy will.

In the following pages, we will see with a new understanding how the Spirituality of the Cross is completely encompassed within one reality: EXERCISING OUR BAPTISMAL PRIESTHOOD; offering to the Father our only valid sacrifice, which is Christ, and offering ourselves in union with him, in the totality of a holocaust.

This is something quite profound and merits serious theological reflection, which will be short, but clear, and within everyone's ability to understand.

SECOND PART

THEOLOGICAL CONSIDERATIONS

CHAPTER ONE

THE PRIESTHOOD OF JESUS

1. JESUS AS VICTIM

In the course of gradual revelation, Jesus first appeared as VICTIM and only later as PRIEST. This is because the historical Jesus was not connected with any known priesthood. This is not just because he did not belong to the tribe of Levi (from which all priests were derived), and not just because he worked with complete independence in respect to the established priestly institutions of the time, but just as importantly, because he harshly criticized the religious leaders of his time. Consequently, he was rejected and put to death by the high priests of Israel. Thus it was difficult for the first Christians to think of Jesus as a priest, let alone a high priest.

On the other hand, the prophet entrusted with announcing the arrival of the Messiah presented Jesus from the beginning as Victim: He was the "Lamb of God":

"The next day he saw Jesus coming toward him and declared, 'Here is the Lamb of God who takes away the sin of the world.'" (Jn 1:29)

The next day John was there again with two of his followers. When he saw Jesus passing by, he proclaimed, "'Look, there is the Lamb of God!' The disciples of John, upon hearing him say this, followed Jesus" (Jn 1:35-36).

One of the "two followers" of the Baptist was St. John, author of the Book of Revelation and of the fourth Gospel. For him, Jesus always continued to be the "Lamb of God." In these two works, he referred to Jesus in this manner fifteen times.

There is no doubt that when the Baptist calls Jesus "the Lamb of God," he is associating him with the "Servant of God" mentioned by the prophet Isaiah.

"But he was pierced for our offenses, crushed for our sins. Upon him was the chastisement that makes us whole; by his wounds we were healed. We had all gone astray like sheep, each following his own way; but the Lord laid upon him the guilt of us all. Though he was harshly treated, he submitted and opened not his mouth. Like a lamb led to the slaughter or a sheep before the shearers, he was silent and opened not his mouth" (Is 53:5-7).

The expression "Lamb of God" also associates Jesus with the lambs that were sacrificed by the Jews as a means of expiation for their sins, and it especially associates Jesus with the "Paschal Lamb." We see this when Jesus himself chooses the meal in which the paschal lamb was customarily consumed to institute the memorial of his death. Jesus "surrenders his body for us" and "sheds his blood for the forgiveness of sins" (cf. Mt 26:2-28).

Furthermore, the paschal feast was seen as a memorial of the liberation of Israel and it brought to mind that lamb whose blood was put on the lintels of the doors by the Israelites, which thus freed them from death. Therefore, by choosing the paschal feast both to institute the new supper and to die on the cross, Jesus clearly expresses that the sacrifice of the paschal lamb has now become the sacrifice of another victim, the Lamb of God, who takes away the sins of the world and brings about the new redemption of the new people of God.

This is what Paul referred to in his letter to the Christians in Corinth: "Get rid of the old yeast to make of yourselves fresh dough, unleavened loaves, as it were; Christ our Passover has been sacrificed" (1Co 5:7).

Finally, the first covenant or pact with God had been sealed by the blood of a sacrifice, as is revealed in the book of Exodus: "Then he (Moses) took the blood and sprinkled it on the people saying, 'This is the blood of the covenant which the Lord has made with you'" (Ex 24:8).

As Jesus offered the wine of that symbolic sacrificial supper (the Lord's Supper) to the disciples, he stated, "This is my blood, with which is sealed the new covenant and which will be shed on behalf of many for the forgiveness of sins" (Mt 26:28).

The author of the Letter to the Hebrews summarizes Jesus' mission as victim in this manner:

"Since the law [of Moses] had only a shadow of the good things to come and no real image of them, it was never able to perfect the worshippers by the same sacrifices offered continually year after year. Were matters otherwise, the priests would have stopped offering them, for the worshippers, once cleansed, would have no sin on their conscience. But through those sacrifices there came only a yearly recalling of sins, because it is impossible for the blood of bulls and goats to take sins away. Wherefore, on coming into the world, Jesus said:

"Sacrifice and offering you did not desire

But a body you have prepared for me.

Holocausts and sin offerings you took no delight in.

Then I said, 'As is written of me in the book,

I have come to do your will, O God'" (He 10:1-7).

First he says that God doesn't want sacrifices of animals to take away sin, even though these are offered according to the law (cf. Heb 10:8). He then says, "Here I am, I come to do your will." That is, he takes away the old sacrifices and offers a new one in their place. God has accepted us as his own because Jesus did the will of God by offering his own body as a sacrifice once and for all. By means of this one offering, those who now belong to God were made definitively perfect (cf. He 10:9-10).

It is important that we emphasize that Jesus is an offering or victim presented to the Father, not by the act of being martyred on the cross, but rather by his spiritual disposition to submit himself faithfully to fulfilling the will of the Father. This surrender constitutes perfect love and this obedience of Christ merited our redemption and his glorification. Let us examine the following verses:

1. "My soul is troubled now. Yet what should I say? 'Father, save me from this hour?' But it was for this purpose that I came to this hour. Father, glorify your name" (Jn 12:28).

2. "I shall not go on speaking to you longer; the Prince of this world is at hand. He has no hold on me, but the world must know that I love the Father and I do just as the Father has commanded me. Come then! Let us be on our way" (Jn 14:30-31).

3. "Jesus advanced a little, bent over until his forehead touched the ground, and prayed to God that, if possible, the hour of sorrow might pass by. In his prayer, he said, 'Abba, Father, all things are possible for you. Take this cup away from me, yet not what I want but what you will'" (Mk 14:35).

4. "In the days when he was in the flesh, he offered prayers and supplications with loud cries and tears to God, who was able to save him from death, and he was heard because of his obedience" (He 5:7). God heard him and freed him from death by means of his resurrection and final glorification.

5. "He humbled himself, becoming obedient to death, even death on the Cross. Because of this, God greatly exalted him and bestowed on him the name that is above every other name" (Phil 2:8-9).

By reading these texts, we learn that what is essential regarding the sacrifice of Jesus, and what pleases the Father, is clearly not the suffering of his beloved Son, but rather his loving obedience, which was lived out each day of his life and proved and expressed supremely by his death on a Cross.

In light of this, we comprehend that Jesus is an offering to the Father, and a perfect victim throughout his entire existence. As he himself declared:

"My food is to do the will of him who sent me and to finish his work" (Jn 4:34).

"I came down from heaven not to do my own will but the will of the One who sent me" (Jn 6:38).

"The One who sent me is with me. He has not left me alone, because I do what is pleasing to him" (Jn 8:29).

"No one takes my life from me, but I give it by my own will" (Jn 10:18).

Thus we see that to be a victim means to love the Father unconditionally, and without limits. It means to always do his will because we love him and he loves all of us. To be a victim in union with Jesus does not necessarily mean one dies by martyrdom; it doesn't even mean one suffers a little or a lot. Rather, it signifies that one loves the Father to such an extent that the person is disposed in all things to do the Father's will. To be a victim, according to the Spirituality of the Cross, means to center our lives in the faithful completion of the will of the Father, uniting ourselves to Jesus through faith and through love.

It is important to understand that the offering of Jesus to the Father is not necessarily his death in itself, but rather his love unto death. It is not his pain that is important, but his love, which enables him to accept supreme pain.

That is why Jesus can offer his sacrifice eternally without having to die again, since the eternal offering is that love that had its supreme expression in his martyrdom on the Cross "once for all" (He 10:12).

By the same token, being a victim with Jesus does not mean to suffer, but to love the Father with a love that leads one to brave all things – even death on the cross, if that is the Father's will.

But, in fact, all of us suffer, some more, some less, but without exception. We all carry some cross as we follow Christ. It is an indispensable condition for uniting ourselves to him. How can we imitate Jesus in his obedience even to the Cross, if we don't suffer also through our own obedience? How can we follow him, if not through Calvary? How can the quality of our love be proven, if not in the crucible of suffering? It is the same Jesus who says, "If anyone wishes to be my disciple, let him take up his cross and follow me" (Mt 10:38; Lk 14:27).

But this image of Jesus as victim would be very incomplete if we did not consider that this will of the Father, to which Jesus submits himself completely, is the very salvation of mankind, and that Jesus accepts this mission with an infinite love for all humanity:

"And this is the will of the One who sent me: that I should not lose any of those whom he gave me" (Jn 6:39).

"I am the Good Shepherd. A good shepherd lays down his life for his sheep" (Jn 10:11).

"No one has greater love than this, to lay down one's life for one's friends" (Jn 15:13).

"Christ loved us and gave himself for us as an offering to God, as a pleasing fragrance" (Eph 5:2).

"Christ has loved me and given himself up for me" (Ga 2:20).

"He loves us and has freed us from our sins by his blood" (Rev 1:5).

Thus we see that Jesus surrendered his life, not solely out of obedience to the Father, but also out of love for us, his brothers and sisters. Therefore, to be a victim in union with Christ implies having a generous love for all people, having a great desire for their integral salvation (now and in the age to come). It means having an interior disposition to accept our sufferings which, in union with those of Christ, will serve for the redemption of all humanity, our grand family.

St. Paul understood this clearly when he wrote, "Now I rejoice in my sufferings for your sake and in my flesh I am filling up what is lacking in the afflictions of Christ" (Col 1:24).

If Jesus is the vine and we are the branches (cf. Jn 15), if Jesus is the head of the Church and we are its body (cf. 1Co 12:27), then it is natural that we should participate in his redemptive suffering, not because the Lord's Passion was insufficient, but rather because our union with Jesus is so real that we are destined to participate in the very same paschal redemption with him: sharing in his Cross now, and later, in his glory.

How true it is that the Cross is the entire Gospel expressed in one single letter. The vertical beam points to heaven and represents our relationship with the Father, our surrender to the Father, our love for the Father. The horizontal beam, which signifies the earth, represents our love for our brothers and sisters, our surrender to their interests and needs.

If someone attempts to live the Spirituality of the Cross in a purely vertical sense, that person has not understood anything regarding the mystery of Christ nor what it means to live in union with Jesus as Priest and Victim.

2. JESUS AS ETERNAL HIGH PRIEST

The only biblical document that presents Jesus as priest is the Letter to the Hebrews. The author begins with the Jewish priesthood instituted by God himself. He does this not to assign this same priestly role to Jesus, but rather the contrary, to demonstrate that Jesus supersedes and transcends the priesthood of the first Covenant, and he does this to such an extent that the ancient priesthood has now been abolished; there now exists no other priesthood than that of Christ.

Just what is a priest? He is defined as an intermediary between God and the people. He is the one who prays on behalf of the people, intercedes for their weaknesses and sins, and presents to God the supplications and needs of the faithful. But to be able to do all this, he must offer gifts to God that the people have set apart and dedicated: offerings for sins, offerings of thanksgiving and praise, and offerings of supplication by which we can merit the help of God. Then God blesses his people and bestows sacred gifts on them by means of this very priest, which means "one who gives sacred things."

The author of the Letter to the Hebrews applies this common notion of what constitutes a priest to Jesus, but he elevates it to a celestial and eternal level. Here are some texts that present the essence of this teaching:

"Every high priest is chosen from among men and made their representative before God, to offer gifts and sacrifices for sins" (He 5:1).

"Therefore, since we have a Great High Priest, who has passed through the heavens, Jesus, the Son of God, let us hold fast to our confession. For we do not have a high priest who is unable to sympathize with our weaknesses, but One who has similarly been tested in every way, yet without sin" (He 4:14-15).

"Now he of whom these things are said belonged to a different tribe from which no member ever officiated at the altar. It is clear that Our Lord arose from Judah, and with regard to that tribe, Moses said nothing about priesthood" (He 7:13-14).

"For that reason, Christ did not enter into a sanctuary made by men, a copy of the true one, but into heaven itself, that he might now appear before God on our behalf. Not that he might offer himself repeatedly, as the high priest enters each year into the sanctuary with blood that is not his own; if that were so, he would have had to suffer repeatedly from the foundation of the world. But now once for all he has appeared at the end of the ages to take away sin by his sacrifice. Just as it is appointed that human beings die once, and after this the judgment, so also Christ, offered once to take away the sins of many, will appear a second time, not to take away sin, but to bring salvation to those who eagerly await him" (He 9:24-28).

"But when Christ came as High Priest of the good things that have come to be, passing through the greater and more perfect tabernacle not made by hands, that is, not belonging to this creation, he entered once for all into the sanctuary, not with the blood of goats and calves, but with his own blood, thus obtaining eternal redemption. For if the blood of goats and bulls and the sprinkling of a heifer's ashes can sanctify those who are defiled so that their flesh is cleansed, how much more will the blood of Christ, who through the Eternal Spirit offered himself unblemished to God, cleanse our consciences from dead works to worship the living God" (He 9:11-14).

"It was fitting that we should have such a High Priest: holy, innocent, undefiled, separated from sinners, higher than the heavens. He has no need, as did the high priests, to offer sacrifice day after day, first for his own sins and then for those of the people; he did that once for all when he offered himself" (He 7:26-27).

"The main point of what has been said is this: we have such a High Priest, who has taken his seat at the right hand of the throne of the Majesty in heaven, a minister of the sanctuary and of the true tabernacle that the Lord, not man, set up" (He 8:1-2).

Jesus is eternal High Priest, because by dying on the Cross, he entered into the presence of the Father and offered this act of perfect love by which he accepted death: "Father, into your hands I commend my spirit" (Lk 23:46).

Therefore, as Jesus entered heaven, he left life within the confines of time and passed on to a new mode of existence called eternity, which exists in a moment of fullness that will never end. There is no past, present, or future. There is no living in segments, but rather for all time. In this eternity, Jesus forever became the God-Man who came into the presence of the Father, offering his life as a unique sacrifice for the salvation of the world. In heaven, then, there is a perpetual liturgy, an unceasing worship, an eternal sacrifice – and this is what constitutes the risen Jesus as our sole High Priest.

When we celebrate Mass over and over here on earth, we are not multiplying the eternal sacrifice of Christ, but rather we lower from the heavens to our altars the one unique celestial sacrifice; we are participating in our earthly temples in that unique liturgy which exists in that "sanctuary not belonging to this creation"; we are uniting ourselves in a determined point in time with that worship which exists in the "always" where humanity, glorified by our Redeemer, lives and acts.

Imagine an immense temple in a circular shape that has 365 windows with distinct colors. Our daily attendance of Mass throughout the liturgical year would be similar to the daily poking of our heads through each window to contemplate the same sacrifice of Jesus which is at the center of the temple, always realizing itself in the eternal instant; this being the means by which the Father receives the only perfect worship, the one unique and worthy offering, and the sole and effective intercession.

The priesthood of Christ had its beginning in Bethlehem and its culmination on Calvary, but its actual and definitive reality is in the heavenly sanctuary in the presence of God the Father.

CHAPTER TWO

THE PRIESTHOOD OF MARY

It is clear and evident that God wanted to grant Mary a special and unique participation in the priesthood of Jesus and within the entire mystery of our salvation; she was chosen to give life to the Divine Word, to give him the human nature by which he could carry out his messianic ministry through his redemptive sacrifice.

The Son was not given to Mary so that she could possess him, but rather so that she could give him to us.

When her Son was just forty days old, she went to the temple in Jerusalem to fulfill the requirement of the law that God had given to his people through Moses: "It is written in the law of the Lord, 'Every first-born male that opens the womb shall be consecrated to the Lord'" (Lk 2:23).

"Now there was a man in Jerusalem whose name was Simeon. This man was righteous and devout, awaiting the consolation of Israel, and the Holy Spirit was upon him. It had been revealed to him by the Holy Spirit that he should not see death before he had seen the Messiah of the Lord. Guided by the Holy Spirit, he came into the temple; and when the parents brought in the child Jesus to perform the custom of the law in regard to him, he took him into his arms and blessed God saying, 'Now, Master, you may let your servant go in peace, according to your word, for my eyes have seen your salvation, which you prepared in the sight of all the peoples, a light for revelation to the Gentiles and glory for your people Israel.'"

The Child's father and mother were amazed at what was said about him, and Simeon blessed them and said to Mary, his mother, "Behold, this Child is destined for the fall and rise of many in Israel. He will be a sign that will be contradicted (and you yourself a sword will pierce) so that the thoughts of many hearts may be revealed" (Lk 2:23-35).

All Jewish women would go to the temple to offer their first-born sons to God. It was a beautiful rite, and they would undoubtedly carry it out in a heartfelt manner. But in the case of Mary, it was rather different. She who had conceived this Son by the work of the Holy Spirit, was filled with the Holy Spirit and in the light of "the One who spoke through the prophets," began to grasp that mystery surrounding her extraordinary maternity and the destiny of the fruit of her womb. "Mary kept all these things in her heart" (Lk 2:51).

Thus Mary went to the temple to offer her Son, fully aware of what she was doing. She knew that Jesus was the long awaited Messiah, the one who "would inherit the throne of his ancestor David and whose kingdom would have no end." But she did not know how God would carry out his plan, how Jesus would fulfill his messianic mission. Therefore, she offered her Son to God, so that the Father might work through him according to his will and thus bring about his eternal plan.

Thus we see the Mother taking on her priestly role, offering to God what is truly hers, flesh of her flesh and blood of her blood, son of her womb and of her heart.

She offered the Lamb of God, the Holy Victim, the perfect offering, the same way all priests do today before the altar, but with a much greater right to do so because the offering is an integral part of her. And her offering was more perfect because the holiness of her soul and the immensity of her love were so superior.

God responded to her by means of a prophet who foretold her future and that of her son, "Behold, this child is destined for the fall and rise of many in Israel and to be a sign that will be contradicted, and you yourself a sword will pierce" (Lk 2:35).

God did not want to place any false hope in Mary's heart, and he warned her clearly regarding what her destiny and that of her Son would be and how much she would suffer. Mary began to understand the nature of Jesus' Messianic mission. She knew the Scriptures; she knew what Isaiah had prophesied regarding the mysterious Servant of the Lord, who would show the people the ways of God and would pay the debt of humanity through his own sufferings.

In spite of the prophecy of Simeon, Mary reiterated the offering which she had just made of her son, whom she loved more than her own life, and she reaffirmed her consistent spiritual stance before God: "I am the servant of the Lord." Then "when they had fulfilled all the prescriptions of the law of the Lord, they returned to Galilee, to their own town of Nazareth. The child grew and became strong, filled with wisdom; and the favor of God was upon him" (Lk 2:39-40).

How these words sum up the life of Mary! We all know what it is like for a mother to see her child grow. It is a continual novelty, full of surprises and graces, and it is a continual exchange of love.

Mary saw each day how "Jesus advanced in wisdom and age," but along with the joy that came from an ever more complete and profound dialogue with Jesus, the pain caused by Simeon's announcement was also growing. This pain was now a sword that began to wound her soul and led her to constantly repeat that "Yes" that she had always given to God.

We can barely imagine the delightful relationship that existed between Mary and Jesus when he was an adolescent and a young man. Perhaps it would help if we imagine the relationship between an only son and his mother in some small and isolated village. The child would have had nothing to do with things outside of his home, and in his home there would be hardly anything apart from his mother; and the mother would live only for her son.

We know that Joseph, the beloved spouse of Mary, the loving foster father of Jesus, passed away before Jesus died, because otherwise Jesus would not have given his beloved disciple the task of taking care of his mother. Thus, for several years – we don't know how many – Mary and Jesus lived alone in their house in Nazareth. They would dine together, they would pray together, they would tend to the garden together and talk about God...and as evening fell they would delight in some wonderful conversation over the intimacy of the evening meal. This lady, so simple and poor, enjoyed the greatest of all riches; and that working-class young man had in his home that which was most desirable in the universe...

But the day arrived...that day when Jesus decided to go to John to be baptized and receive the baptism of the Holy Spirit, and the Spirit of God led him to the desert; and Jesus did not return home; and the sword began to penetrate very deeply into the mother's soul....

The two saw each other at the wedding in Cana. They would see each other whenever Jesus passed through Nazareth. One day "someone told him, 'Your Mother and your brothers are standing outside, asking to speak with you' but the family could not come in because the house was inundated with disciples" (Mt 12:47).

Jesus would walk throughout the whole region of Palestine or he would spend a few weeks in Capernaum. His Mother hardly saw him anymore. She would lift up her eyes to heaven and exclaim, "I am the servant of the Lord."

This was the new situation in which she would continually offer her Son to the divine will of God, for the glory of God and the salvation of all people. The offering would become abandonment, and this surrender would transform itself into a sacrifice much more real than that of Abraham.

One night someone came to warn Mary that her Son had just been arrested. What a night that was! Later, the judgment, the calumny, Pilate, the shouting, the injustice, the incredible unexpected sentence.... Later, the encounter in some alleyway: Jesus scourged, spat upon, beaten, with a crown of thorns on his head and his face so swollen....

Mary could not believe what her eyes were seeing.... How can this be? Why? Her son ...her Jesus...! My God, I cannot understand! My God! Why?

She followed him all the way up to Calvary...the soldiers...the hammer, the nails, there naked, hanging on the wood, drowning in pain.... "Standing by the Cross was his mother" (Jn 19:25).

There was the priestly Virgin offering two victims for all of us: her Son and her own crucified heart.

"When Jesus saw his mother and the disciple there whom he loved, he said to his mother, 'Woman, behold your son.' Then he said to his disciple, 'Behold your Mother.' From that hour, the disciple took her into his home" (Jn 19:26-27).

Then two days passed after the burial of Jesus and his mother seemed to be dying of pain. But on the morning of the third day, Mary saw Jesus resurrected. The Gospels tell us nothing of this very intimate and joyful moment, but we can give credence to what St. Teresa of Avila tells us in her autobiography: "The Lord told me that upon his resurrection, he visited our Lady because she was distraught, and her pain was so deep that even upon seeing him, she could not readily collect herself to be able to fully delight in this joyous occasion. Thus it was necessary to spend much time with her."

The last mention of Mary in the New Testament is when she was gathered with the apostles and the first believers in the upper room at Pentecost: "All these devoted themselves with one accord to prayer, together with some women, and Mary the mother of Jesus, and his brothers" (Ac 1:14).

At that time Mary was close to fifty years of age and tradition assures us that she lived even longer in the company of St. John.

Jesus is our life and Mary gave him to us. Mary gave us life in Jesus, and one who gives life is a mother. Mary is our mother because God chose to associate her intimately with the mystery of our "new birth in Christ." Illuminated by the Holy Spirit, she became more and more aware of this call to universal maternity. She accepted her years in solitude on earth in order to be, the principal example of faith, love and humility among Christ's disciples, as well as the faithful witness of all that pertains to Jesus.

The Church, guided by the Holy Spirit, has taught us as a dogma of our faith that one day Mary was taken up into heaven body and soul, as the first of those redeemed through the merits of Christ.

What then does Mary do in heaven, if not glorify God and intercede for her children on earth? Moreover, what better way is there to do this than by offering the Father her perfect worship, her perfect host, her perfect offering, her divine Son?

Just as the glorified Jesus remains forever as the Eternal High Priest, so also Mary, taken up into heaven, participates with greater rights than anyone else in that joyful Eucharist, which takes place in that sublime temple where the blessed dwell forever.

That is why those of us here on earth, who offer Christ under the species of bread to the Father, unite ourselves with the eternal "presentation" by which Mary offers her first born to God, not in the temple in Jerusalem, but in the definitive temple where the resplendent presence of God is manifested.

CHAPTER THREE

OUR PRIESTHOOD

Three months after leaving Egypt, the descendants of Israel arrived at a mountain in the Sinai desert and they camped there. It was there that Yahweh spoke to Moses and ordered him:

"Thus shall you say to the house of Jacob; tell the Israelites: 'If you hearken to my voice and keep my covenant, you shall be my special possession, dearer to me than all other people, though all the earth is mine. You shall be to me a kingdom of priests, a holy nation'" (Ex 19:3, 5-6).

As we know, the first covenant was only transitory and God brought about a new covenant, new and eternal, through Christ, from which was born the *new Israel of God*, the definitive People that belong to him. And all the promises made in the old covenant were perfectly fulfilled in the new covenant. That is why St. Peter wrote to the Christians recently converted from paganism:

"Like living stones let yourselves be built into a spiritual house to be a holy priesthood to offer spiritual sacrifices acceptable to God through Jesus Christ. You are a chosen race, a royal priesthood, a holy nation, a people of his own. Once you were 'no people' but now you are God's people" (1 P 2:5,9).

In the book of Revelation, St. John tells us: "Christ loved us and has freed us from our sins by his blood, who has made us into a kingdom, priests for his God and Father" (Rev 1:5).

Later on in the same book, he presents to us the image of the blessed kneeling before the Lamb, singing the new song: "For you were slain and with your blood you purchased for God those from every tribe and tongue, people and nation. You made them a kingdom and priests for our God, and they will reign on earth" (Rev 5:9).

In these texts the book of Revelation clearly teaches us that all who were redeemed by Christ were *purchased for God*, that is, consecrated to his service; these now constitute a *chosen family*, just as in ancient times the tribe of Levi was chosen as a priestly tribe. These people (redeemed by Christ) are now a *temple of living stones*; that is to say, they are consecrated to divine worship, as all temples are, and therefore they are *a holy priesthood*, not called to offer animal sacrifices, but rather *to offer spiritual sacrifices acceptable to God through Jesus Christ* (1 P 2:5).

These texts refer to the BAPTISMAL PRIESTHOOD, also called the COMMON PRIESTHOOD OF THE FAITHFUL, concerning which Vatican II speaks thus:

> Christ, Our Lord and High Priest, taken from among men, made his new people 'a kingdom of priests for God the Father.'
>
> The baptized are consecrated as a spiritual temple and a holy priesthood by means of their rebirth and their anointing by the Holy Spirit, which is realized in Baptism (*Lumen Gentium*, n. 10).

We can identify five realities by which Jesus has made us a priestly people:

1. Our privilege to have access to God to offer him worship.

2. Our investiture to offer a perfect sacrifice to God.

3. Our union with the Victim who is pleasing to God.

4. Our function as intermediaries and co-redeemers.

5. The ministerial aspect of the priesthood.

We are going to explain each of these realities separately:

1. OUR PRIVILEGE TO ENTER THE HOLY OF HOLIES

The priesthood of the first covenant was based on a system of respectful separations which kept the common man at a great distance from an "inaccessible God." Women could enter up to a certain limit within the temple. The men could go only a little further inside. The priests would take turns entering into the "holy place" to burn incense. Only the high priest could pass through the veil of the sanctuary and enter the "holy of holies" and this he did only once a year. He would enter the "inner sanctuary" and offer the blood from a sacrificed animal in atonement for the sins of the people. But even he could not enter into the presence of God. It was believed that only the life of the victim being offered would reach the presence of the "Most High" as an intercessory offering.

However, upon Jesus' death "the veil of the sanctuary was torn in two from top to bottom" (Mk 15:38). From then on, the entrance to the "holy place" remained open for everyone, that is to say, all now had free access to God: because the blood of the Son purified us from all stain of sin, it sanctified us with his Spirit and it made us worthy to offer worship to God confidently as sons and daughters calling upon God as our Father.

No ancient priest ever had such a privilege. However, through Christian baptism we are "baptized into Christ and clothed with Christ" (Ga 3:27). Jesus says, "I am the vine and you are the branches" (Jn 15:5) and by uniting ourselves to his very life, he also unites us to his praise, to his adoration, and to his worship; in other words, he has "made us a royal priesthood for his God and Father." The liturgical formula expresses this, as "Through him, with him, in him, in the unity of the Holy Spirit, all glory and honor is yours, almighty Father, for ever and ever."

This is the culmination of the redemptive work of Jesus: to be able to transform man, who is sinful and separated from God, into man who is consecrated to divine worship; not just by removing the obstacles which separated God from man so man can have free access to God, but above all, through an indispensible union with Jesus himself who is, in essence, the One who worships the Father. That is why it is written that "by one offering he has made perfect forever those who are being consecrated" (He 10:14).

2. OUR RIGHT TO OFFER GOD THE ONE UNIQUE SACRIFICE

The second reality which defines all Christians as priests is the fact that all who are baptized have received a holy right by which they can offer as though their own offering, the unique sacrifice of all Christian altars, which is Christ himself.

One priestly action is the "Consecration," or transformation of the bread and wine into the real presence of Jesus Christ. In this instance, only the ordained priest serves as an instrument of Our Lord Jesus, who becomes the essence of that bread and wine, while leaving their appearance intact.

The second priestly action within the Eucharistic Sacrifice is the "offering of the Victim." In this, all the people present participate. The minister, together with each of the faithful gathered around, exercise their baptismal priesthood, then more than ever.

Jesus makes himself present in a state that reflects his immolation on the Cross. The bread signifies his body separated from his blood, and the wine signifies his blood separated from his body, just as it happened at the moment of his sacrifice, when his blood poured out of his body.

And thus, the eternal offering of heavenly worship is actualized in the midst of the priestly congregation, so that each individual makes this his or her OFFERING, and presents this to the

Father through the prayers of the liturgy:

> Father, upon celebrating the memorial of the death and resurrection of your Son, we offer you the sacrifice of perfect reconciliation that you yourself PUT IN OUR HANDS" (Eucharistic Prayer for Reconciliation).

> Therefore, as we celebrate the memorial of his Death and Resurrection, we offer you, Lord, the Bread of Life and the Chalice of salvation, giving thanks that you have held us worthy TO BE IN YOUR PRESENCE AND MINISTER TO YOU" (Eucharistic Prayer II).

> Remember Lord, those of us gathered here, whose faith and devotion are known to you. For them, we offer you this sacrifice of praise, or THEY OFFER IT FOR THEMSELVES" (Eucharistic Prayer I).

> This is why the priest says: "Pray, my brothers and sisters, that MY SACRIFICE AND YOURS may be acceptable to God, the Almighty Father.

We cannot deny that the most important moment of our priestly function is when we offer Jesus to the Father, the Son who pleases him, transformed into our sacrament, our offering, our victim. It is then that we give the only worthy worship to God and when we exercise our mediation in favor of others in the most effective manner, since we intercede for the living and the dead in the name of Jesus Christ, who told us: "Whatever you ask the Father in my name, he will give you" (Jn 16:23).

3. OUR UNION WITH CHRIST AS VICTIM

Our participation in the priesthood of Jesus does not consist solely in being able to offer him to the Father as our offering, but also in being able to offer ourselves together with Jesus as victims pleasing to God. That is why St. Paul tells us:

"I urge you therefore, brothers, by the mercies of God, to offer your bodies as a living sacrifice holy and pleasing to God, your spiritual worship. This is the true worship that you should offer" (Ro 12:1).

There are two ways in which we offer ourselves to the Father together with Jesus:

    A. In the Eucharistic Celebration

    B. In our Daily Life

We shall further clarify these two concepts:

A. *In the Eucharistic Celebration*

St. Cyprian (3rd century) wrote to the Christians of his time: "The sacrifice of the Lord cannot be celebrated in its entire holiness if our own offering is not in conformity to the one of Christ in his passion."

That is why the Eucharistic liturgy leads us to be victims with Christ in the same sacrifice.

Look, O Lord, upon the Sacrifice which you yourself have provided for your Church, and grant in your loving kindness to all who partake of this one Bread and one Chalice that, gathered into one body by the Holy Spirit, they may truly become a living sacrifice in Christ to the praise of your glory (Eucharistic Prayer IV).

> Look, we pray, upon the oblation of your Church and, recognizing the sacrificial Victim by whose death you willed to reconcile us to yourself, grant that we, who are nourished by the Body and Blood of your Son and filled with his Holy Spirit, may become one body, one spirit in Christ. May he make of us an eternal offering to you (Eucharistic Prayer III).

To be a victim with Jesus in the sacrament of the Eucharist means that we offer ourselves to the Father spiritually united with Christ, and with his same unconditional surrender.

This is what Pope Pius XI teaches us in his encyclical *Miserentissimus Redemptor:*

"In the Eucharistic sacrifice, the minister and the faithful should unite their own immolation to that of Christ, offering themselves 'as living hosts, holy, and pleasing to God.' For the wisdom of God has desired that *what is lacking in the Passion of Christ for the sake of the Church be fulfilled in us.*"

Theologians tell us that the sacrifice of Jesus consists in his own sacrifice as well as that of all humanity, given that Jesus acted as our leader, our representative, our High Priest.

Jesus then offers his life together with our poor lives, our poor works, and our poor tears. But it is necessary that we place ourselves in his hands; because to immolate himself, his will was sufficient. But for him to immolate us with himself, our consent is necessary. This is how we come to form "one sole body and one sole spirit" with Christ.

If our baptismal priesthood does not lead us to be victims with Christ, it is because we do not understand the priesthood of Christ, in which the victim being offered is always the same as the one who offers it.

And whoever exercises the priestly ministry will be able to sanctify others with his spiritual gift, but will not sanctify himself if he does not become a single victim with Christ during the celebration of the holy mysteries.

B. *In our Daily Life*

We have already said that to be a victim is nothing less than to surrender oneself unconditionally to the will of God. Thus we cannot separate our sacramental participation with Christ as Victim from our existential and daily participation in his obedience to the Father. In any other manner, our Eucharistic offering would be absolutely false, an unacceptable hypocrisy.

From the beginning, our Christian life consists in voluntarily dying so that God's most loving will can be realized in our lives:

"Put to death, then, the parts of you that are earthly" (Col 3:5).

"By the spirit you put to death the deeds of the body" (Ro 8:13).

"We know our old self was crucified with him, so that our old sinful body might be done away with. If, then, we have died with Christ, we believe that we shall also live with him" (Rom 6:6, 8).

Scripture also says:

"To keep the law is a great oblation, and he who observes the commandments sacrifices a peace offering. In works of charity, one offers fine flour, and when he gives alms he presents his sacrifice of praise. To refrain from evil pleases the Lord and to avoid injustice is atonement" (Si 35:1-3).

The Second Vatican Council summarized this doctrine as follows:

It is through the sacraments and the exercise of the virtues that the sacred nature and organic structure of the priestly community is brought into operation.

This is in order that through all those works which are those of the Christian, they may offer spiritual sacrifices and proclaim the power of him who has called them out of darkness into his marvelous light.

Therefore all the disciples of Christ should present themselves as a living sacrifice, holy and pleasing to God" (*Lumen Gentium*, nn. 10 and 11).

This is a very rich teaching. It is like the legendary magical rock that turned everything that it touched into gold; all of our works, even the least significant, are converted into worthy and pleasing offerings to the Father, because they are done in an intimate union with Jesus Christ. That is why St. Paul gives us this advice:

"So whether you eat or drink, or whatever you do, do everything in the name of Jesus Christ and for the glory of God" (1Co 10:31).

This doctrine shows us the shortest route leading to the goal of all spirituality: our transformation into Christ. And whoever follows it faithfully, can soon echo the words of St. Paul: "Yet I live, no longer I, but Christ who lives in me" (Ga 2:20).

It is sad that we waste our lives so full of labor, toil, and suffering; it is tragic that all this derives no merit, no spiritual richness, just because we did not convert each and every one of our moments into an offering to the Father in union with Jesus Christ.

The life of a poor beggar who has truly made himself a victim with Jesus is worth more than that of a king or a pope who did not offer his life to the Father in union with Christ.

"For whoever wishes to save his life will lose it, but whoever loses his life for my sake and that of the Gospel will save it" (Lk 9:24).

4. OUR FUNCTION AS CO-REDEEMERS

Inasmuch as we participate in the priesthood and sacrifice of Christ, it is impossible for us to be excluded from the horizontal dimensions of his mission.

There are numerous references in scripture that point to the salvation of humanity as the main objective of the Incarnation, the priesthood, and the sacrifice of Christ:

"This saying is trustworthy and deserves full acceptance: that Christ Jesus came into the world to save sinners" (1Ti 1:15).

"Moreover, we have seen and testify that the Father sent his Son as savior of the world" (1 Jn 4:14).

"In him, we have redemption by his blood, the forgiveness of transgressions, in accord with the riches of his grace" (Eph 1:7).

"Through Christ, God has reconciled all things for him, making peace by the blood of his Cross" (Col 1:20).

"Christ entered once for all into the sanctuary, not with the blood of goats and calves, but with his own blood, thus obtaining eternal redemption" (He 9:12).

Without a doubt, we have well understood the meaning of these texts.

And so we ask: If we are truly united with Jesus, forming with him a single vine, a single body, a single priesthood and a single Victim, then how could we possibly think that we have nothing to do with the redemptive aspect of the mission of Christ?

Everyone's participation in the salvation of all people is nothing less than the concrete application of the dogma of the "communion of saints" (that is, of the faithful) that we affirm in our Creed. This reality consists in the sharing of the spiritual goods among all people who form the family of God, the brotherhood of the Church, the Christian community. The works that each person performs in union with CHRIST, always result in the benefit of all: the same way that the good health of each one of our bodily organs benefits the well being of the entire body. This communion, or communication, or participation, of each one of us in the welfare of our brothers and sisters in faith is a dogma; it is the foundation of our co-redemptive role, which is the horizontal dimension of our baptismal priesthood.

All this is a consequence of another beautiful truth: All the mysteries of Christ have their consummation in each one of us, because after realizing these mysteries in himself, Christ continually realizes them in his mystical body, in his renewed people, in his holy Church. Jesus has incorporated us into himself in such a real manner that by being united with him, we have become crucified with him, dead to the world, offered to the Father, sanctified by the same Spirit, resurrected into his very life, and seated with him on the heavenly throne (Eph 2:6).

"For those he foreknew he also predestined to be conformed to the image of his Son, that he might be the firstborn among many brothers" (Ro 8:29).

Now, if we say that all the mysteries of Christ have their consummation in each and every one of us because we are his mystical body, it means that we are truly incorporated into the mystery of his redemptive Passion. By being victims with him, we participate in his saving obedience and liberating Cross, just as we also await participation in his glory.

In light of all this, how fitting are the words of St. Paul:

"Now I rejoice in my sufferings for your sake, and in my flesh I am filling up what is lacking in the afflictions of Christ on behalf of his body, which is the Church" (Col 1:24).

5. THE MINISTERIAL PRIESTHOOD

In the preface of the Chrism Mass of Jesus Christ, Eternal High Priest, we have a wonderful summary of all that we want to expound upon:

> It is truly right and just, our duty and our salvation,
> always and everywhere to give you thanks,
> Lord, holy Father, almighty and eternal God.
>
> For by the anointing of the Holy Spirit
> you made your Only Begotten Son
> High Priest of the new and eternal covenant,
> and by your wondrous design were pleased to decree
> that his one Priesthood should continue in the Church.
>
> For Christ not only adorns with a royal priesthood
> the people he has made his own,
> but with a brother's kindness he also chooses men
> to become sharers in his sacred ministry
> through the laying on of hands.
>
> They are to renew in his name
> the sacrifice of human redemption,
> to set before your children the paschal banquet,
> to lead your holy people in charity,
> to nourish them with the word
> and strengthen them with the Sacraments.
>
> As they give up their lives for you
> and for the salvation of their brothers and sisters,

they strive to be conformed to the image of Christ himself
and offer you a constant witness of faith and love.

And so, Lord, with all the Angels and Saints,
we, too, give you thanks, as in exultation we acclaim:

The Second Vatican Council clarified very well the relationship that exists between the baptismal priesthood and the ordained priesthood:

Though they differ from one another in essence and not only in degree, the common priesthood of the faithful and the ministerial or hierarchical priesthood are nonetheless interrelated; each of them, in its own special way is a participation in the one priesthood of Christ. The ministerial priest, by the sacred power he enjoys, teaches and rules the priestly people; acting in the person of Christ, he makes present the Eucharistic sacrifice, and offers it to God in the name of all the people. But the faithful, in virtue of their royal priesthood, join in the offering of the Eucharist. They likewise exercise that priesthood in receiving the sacraments, in prayer and thanksgiving, in the witness of a holy life, and by self-denial and active charity" (*Lumen Gentium*, n. 10).

The Magisterium of the Church has always seen the bishops and the priests who collaborate with them as the legitimate successors of the Apostles elected by Christ to continue his saving mission.

"[Jesus] went up the mountain and summoned those whom he wanted and they came to him. He appointed twelve whom he also named apostles, that they might be with him and he might send them forth to preach and to have authority to drive out demons" (Mk 3:13-

16).

These twelve formed a small community that surrounded Christ. They accompanied him everywhere and he called them friends because he had told them the secrets of the Father.

After the resurrection, Jesus allowed them to see him so that they could be his witnesses. He gave them the power to forgive sins and he ordered them to make disciples of all peoples, baptizing them in the name of the Father, and of the Son, and of the Holy Spirit.

And by the "laying on of hands" the Holy Spirit has, throughout the ages, continued to consecrate those whom the Lord has chosen to carry on his apostolic ministry.

However, the priestly ministry is not a definitive reality, but rather transitory and temporal, given that in heaven there are no sacraments, no need for forgiveness of sins, no preaching, nor any form of mediation.

On the contrary, the baptismal priesthood is definitive and will last forever, because the priestly people will always adore the Father and give him eternal worship, offering to him the one sacrifice in the celestial sanctuary.

The exercise of the ministerial priesthood can only have an eternal repercussion if it is exercised in union with the spiritual priesthood; that is, if the priest lives united to Christ in a living sacrifice of himself, becoming an offering to God and a servant to his brothers and sisters.

Otherwise he would be like a channel through which water flows, yet remains empty. Only integrally living his baptismal and ministerial priesthoods will a priest be like a fountain, pouring out living water from its source of plenty.

CHAPTER FOUR

THE CHAIN OF LOVE

We have left this theme for the end because it concerns itself with a concrete way of living all that we have learned thus far.

On March 27, 1906, two days after the grace of the mystical incarnation, the Lord spoke to Conchita in this way:

"'You see, you are going to make a chain. Every hour of your life shall be a golden link of this chain. I want this chain to remain unbroken until your death. I shall choose many other souls that will, without interruption, continue to add more links to this chain that I want you to start.'"

Gradually, the Lord continued clarifying for Conchita the meaning of this chain made of golden links. From the beginning of April until June 21st, the Lord spoke to Conchita several times, telling her to fill each hour of her life loving God and loving others. He said her love would be a source of all the virtues. That is why this practice became known as the "Chain of Love."

But on June 21st, Jesus explained to Conchita that this practice consisted not only in offering that constant love to God, but above all, in offering Jesus himself to the Father, and in union with Jesus, offering one's own life, a life transformed by love through the action of the Holy Spirit.

June 21st: "The Lord told me: 'In a certain sense you are a priest because you have within you the Victim of Calvary and of the Eucharist, whom you should offer continuously to the eternal Father for the salvation of the world. Alone, what can you accomplish? However, united with me, you and thousands of other souls can continue the work of the salvation of the world, because you offer as a price the merits of the Word Incarnate.'

"'Yes, my Jesus, I now understand that only by offering you can I fulfill my mission of the salvation of souls.'

"'Offer me and offer yourself in union with me to the eternal Father for his glory and for the salvation of the world. You have the sublime mission of priesthood. You shall also be an altar upon which I will offer myself to the Father. And at the same time, you shall be a victim that will be consumed along with the one Victim who can save the world.

"'Now you understand why these hours are rich like the golden links of a chain: Because they are of divine essence and because they are not made by you, but by the merits of the Word made flesh.

"'You must understand well that the works of humans, no matter how holy these are, will have absolutely no value before God unless they are united with me.'"

These words of Jesus are not new, as he had already said them at the Last Supper, when he spoke to his disciples:

"Remain in me, as I remain in you. Just as a branch cannot bear fruit on its own unless it remains on the vine, so neither can you unless you remain in me.

"I am the vine, you are the branches. Whoever remains in me and I in him will bear much fruit, because without me you can do nothing" (Jn 15:4-5).

This doctrine is basic to the Spirituality of the Cross: It is the constant and always growing spiritual union with Jesus, a unique fountain of all divine treasures.

After putting these teachings into practice, Conchita wrote:

June 22nd: "I have begun to offer Jesus to the Eternal Father, just as Jesus told me to do; I do this frequently for the salvation of the world. And how content and empowered I feel having this celestial treasure I can use for the good of others! Now my thirst for saving souls shall be quenched because I am certain that with this treasure I can obtain the graces that others need.

"Now I understand why the links of the chain are made of pure gold. Why not, if in them is he who is all love! Now I can be happy despite all my miseries, because it is not I who purchases, who works, who lives, but rather Jesus in me, God doing everything from within his poor creature."

On July 12th, the Lord persisted with the same theme: "May your heart be an altar upon which my sacrifice is constantly offered without being consumed. While you live, offer me to the Father every moment of your life, for I am the 'Victim of all altars.' But at the same time, offer yourself as well, because in this consists the true priesthood: to be a victim with the Victim. May your life be pure, because this calling to this priestly role is higher than that of the angels."

In Conchita's spiritual diary, we find the following dialogue written on October 20, 1907:

"'But my Jesus, how am I supposed to offer you CONSTANTLY to the Father, since no matter how hard I try, there are still moments when I forget?'

"'Whoever loves me remembers me, and the more you love me, the more frequently you will remember me.'

"'Furthermore, it is not necessary to use words to offer me to the Father. It is enough to have a simple interior gaze with this intention, full of love and tenderness for all people. This is enough for the Father to lavish graces upon the soul that offers me, and to dispense these same graces upon all humanity.'

"'But Lord, doesn't it please you when I offer you to the Father through the words of my prayer?'

"'Yes, I like that. But human speech is not always necessary; what flows from the heart is enough. Thus you will see that what I am asking of you is actually easier. Simply live a pure life, detached from earthly matters, offering me to the Father and offering yourself with me for the salvation of the world. And in this priestly action, forget yourself and just love, adore, and unite yourself to me.'"

A year and a half later, the Lord spoke anew regarding the Chain of Love:

"I want you to offer yourself frequently in union with me, and above all, to do this when you suffer, saying these words: THIS IS MY BODY; THIS IS MY BLOOD. That way, you will offer yourself completely to the Father united to me, because you also are host and victim.

"Unite yourself to me more and more, as if forming one single body and blood, and one immolation alone, for all people. Consent to live my life, giving yourself to others as I gave of myself and for the same cause: for the glory of My Father. Offer me and offer yourself in union with Mary, who was the first priest and victim united with me.

"This is the Chain of Love that must continue forever: a priesthood of souls that want to be victims with me for all time; souls that live my life and who, innocent and pure, offer themselves for the sinful souls of the world.

"That is why I want you to repeat with me: THIS IS MY BODY; THIS IS MY BLOOD; and moved by the love that the Holy Spirit pours forth into your heart, surrender to the Father, disposed to do all that he asks of you."

July 6, 1916: The Lord spoke to Conchita: "This is the goal and the essence of the Works of the Cross: A joining of souls that offer me and offer themselves to the Father for the sake of the world; victims with the One Victim, members of my body, and priests within my priesthood.

"It is not that my sacrifice is insufficient. It is that the essence of my Gospel is that all be ONE with me. This is the supreme goal of the Word made flesh, of the Eucharist, of the action of the Holy Spirit in the Church."

April 28, 1917: "I want the divine Victim to be offered to heaven not just in stone temples, but in the living temples of the Holy Spirit. I also want those doing the offering to be hosts and victims with me.

"Through the sacrament of the Eucharist, I intend to transform all into me. That is why it should not surprise you that I ask all people, united to me, to offer themselves to the Father while saying: 'This is my Body; This is my Blood.'

"When Christians truly become one body with mine, one blood with mine, one heart with mine, and one sacrifice with mine, then the face of the world will change and the Father will be glorified by all humanity. May all people DO THIS IN MEMORY OF ME."

Finally, I would like to quote some lines that refer to the Lord's ministers: "Ask, ask that my priests practice my true priesthood, by offering themselves together with the One Victim that they offer on the altar. Only in this manner do they truly participate in my priesthood, because I am Priest and Victim."

The entire doctrine of the Chain of Love can be summed up in these few words which we find numerous times in the writings of Conchita: OFFER ME AND OFFER YOURSELF.

We have seen that the sacrifice of Jesus is eternal and it is actualized constantly in the "sanctuary that is not of this creation" as well as on our altars across the world from the "setting of the sun to its rising!" Therefore, there is nothing that can impede our spirit and faith from uniting us as much as possible to the constant oblation offered by Jesus, thus exercising our baptismal priesthood. This is the innovation of the Chain of Love: make each hour of our lives into a Mass that will be continually and spiritually offered for the rest of our lives, like an unbroken chain.

Certainly, our union with Jesus Christ is lived out in different ways, considering the distinct schools of spirituality; the characteristic way of living the Spirituality of the Cross is to unite ourselves very closely with Jesus as Priest and Victim.

As we have said, this constant spiritual offering of Jesus and with Jesus transcends the external actions of every moment of our lives. Otherwise, it would not be authentic. In this aspect, the Chain of Love can be summarized by the words of St. Paul in his letter to the Colossians: "And whatever you do, in word or deed, do everything in the name of the Lord Jesus, giving thanks to the Father through him" (Col 3:17).

I believe that anyone who wishes to live the Chain of Love should, at least in the beginning, make a concrete plan of how to offer Jesus and offer oneself. To this end, I recommend the prayer that is found in the manuals for those who belong to the Works of the Cross. Conchita composed this prayer originally, but with time it has been revised somewhat. This is the way it currently appears in our book of intercessions:

"Holy Father, through the hands of Mary, I offer you as victim the Incarnate Word in whom you are well pleased. And moved by the love that the Holy Spirit pours forth into our hearts, I offer myself continuously as victim in union with Jesus, imploring graces for the world and for the Church, and especially for priests. Jesus, Savior of all mankind, save them!"

We shall briefly analyze each part of this prayer:

HOLY FATHER: It is an expression given us by Jesus himself. That is how he addressed his Father (cf. Jn 17:11).

THROUGH THE HANDS OF MARY: That is, uniting myself to her intentions, which are so much wiser than mine; uniting myself to her love, which is so much grander than mine; uniting myself to her priesthood, to her worship, to her thanksgiving, to her maternal intercession for the sake of all. This means desiring that upon offering the "Lamb that is unblemished" my hands stained by sin shall not be seen, but rather, that what will appear will be the pure and holy hands of my Mother.

I OFFER YOU AS VICTIM THE INCARNATE WORD IN WHOM YOU ARE WELL PLEASED: These words make us aware that our offering will always be accepted, will be pleasing, will always be adequate to give the worship to God which he deserves, and that our offering will be efficacious in obtaining forgiveness for all.

AND MOVED BY THE LOVE THAT THE HOLY SPIRIT POURS FORTH INTO OUR HEARTS, I OFFER MYSELF CONTINUOUSLY AS VICTIM IN UNION WITH JESUS: With these words (taken from Ro 5:5) we express our intimate desire and our firm decision to allow ourselves to be guided and moved by the Holy Spirit in exercising this aspect of our baptismal priesthood, namely, the offering of ourselves in union with Jesus, who, "moved by the Holy Spirit, offered himself unblemished to God" (He 9:14).

IMPLORING GRACES FOR THE WORLD AND FOR THE CHURCH: These words make us turn our spiritual eyes, with love and tenderness, toward our brothers and sisters, who like us are weak and sinful, but who live in search of the Supreme Good that is not always known but always deeply desired.

ESPECIALLY FOR PRIESTS: With this last petition, we fulfill the wish that Our Lord expressed to his servant Conchita many times: that we pray for our priests. This is how Jesus expressed the special love he has for those who have desired to be consecrated to him and for God's people. Jesus also expressed the urgent need that the Church has to depend on holy priests who can continue the mission of Christ in the world.

A shorter way of expressing this could be: My Father, in union with my Blessed Mother, I offer you Jesus, and with him, I offer myself to you forever.

After using a verbal formula for some time, it will become a habit to constantly offer the Word Incarnate and ourselves without a further need for words or thoughts. It will be sufficient to lift up our spirits in the presence of the Father in an attitude of filial love, and to offer him a "Yes" which encompasses all.

CHAPTER V

THE QUALITIES OF A VICTIM

Throughout Conchita's writings, the Lord asks those who wish to be victims with him to cultivate three virtues in their lives: love, purity, and a disposition to sacrifice.

Above all else we are to cultivate LOVE, because this is what unites us to the person of Jesus. This personal union is the essential condition to become acceptable offerings.

Moreover, love is the one thing that gives value to all of our oblations: "If I hand my body over so that I may boast but do not have love, I gain nothing" (1Co 13:3).

It's about the love for the Father and for one's brothers and sisters. This love is also about that infinite love that moved Christ to offer himself; this love is the Holy Spirit: "Christ ... through the eternal Spirit, offered himself unblemished to God" (He 9:14).

That is why a devotion to the Holy Spirit is not something incidental or peripheral in the Spirituality of the Cross, but is central and essential to that spirituality.

PURITY: It is said that something is made of PURE gold when the gold of the object is not mixed with other metals. It is said that a soul is PURE when it does not contain other ambitions, other desires, other ideals, other yearnings, except for God: may his name be glorified, may his kingdom come, may his will be done in us and in all his creatures.

Purity does not imply just a renunciation of lust but also of all sin, all that is contrary to the will of God: pride, vanity, hatred, envy, selfishness, anger, sloth, etc.

We can never reach perfect purity in our lives. It is necessary to always ask God to continue to heal our interior infirmity more and more of so many evil tendencies that make us unworthy to be offerings to God.

But notice, we don't have to be perfect to be acceptable offerings. If that were so, nobody could dare offer himself or herself as an oblation to God, who is all holy. The only thing God asks of us is our total surrender to him, that we not interfere with the saving and healing action that his love pours out upon us.

Remember that God was well pleased with the meager dirty coins the widow offered to him, not because they were of great value, but because they were all she had (Lk 21: 1-4). Understand, then, that God does not demand that your offering be rich and beautiful, but rather that your offering be total: an offering of you yourself, as you are, and as much as you can give. The rest is up to God, and he will make you PURE. This will be a process that will last your entire life and will be finished in heaven. The purity that Christ asks of you now is your total surrender.

The profound reason we can now be an offering pleasing to God despite our human limitations is because Christ has incorporated us into himself, as the humble drop of water that is mixed with the wine during the Mass, a drop which becomes wine and then becomes Christ and is offered to God.

For this reason, the Spirituality of the Cross, even though it is radical and demanding, is for everyone; as is Christ, who did not come to look for saints, but sinners.

Archbishop Martínez said it well: "The light of dawn is the same as the light at noon, since it comes from the same sun. In the same manner, our transformation into Christ is essentially the same from our baptism to our highest level of sanctity; it just varies in degree and quality. Therefore, if you are one of the baptized, *it is not you who lives, but Christ who lives in you* and you can now be a pleasing offering to the Father if your surrender is sincere."

SACRIFICE: This is an essential aspect of the Spirituality of the Cross. It consists in loving the Cross of Christ, not because it implies suffering, but because of the conviction that it is the best path to attain purity, understood as total surrender; and love, understood as the strongest and most indestructible union.

The disposition to sacrifice, that is to say, to suffer with love and for love all that God desires, is the secret to perseverance. Without this disposition of the spirit, all suffering, which is inevitable, is converted to stumbling blocks and insurmountable obstacles in our journey toward God. But if we have the disposition to sacrifice for love, all endeavors, all pain and all sufferings are converted into an opportunity for obedience to the will of God and for purification and spiritual growth, and for identification with Jesus Christ.

Finally, in regard to the Chain of Love (April 2, 1906) Conchita tells us that the Lord gave her fourteen rules, as a spiritual program whose main objective is to advance on our journey of transformation into Christ, which is essential for living this "Chain."

Each rule should be practiced during one full month with total diligence. At the end of each day, we should make a brief examination of conscience to see if we have applied the rule successfully. Here are the fourteen rules:

1. Practice true humility.

2. Be pure of mind and body.

3. Be a person of prayer.

4. Practice self-effacement and modesty.

5. Live the poverty of Christ.

6. Forget oneself so as to think only of Jesus.

7. Practice detachment from all earthly affections.

8. Love the Mother of Jesus and imitate her example.

9. Do everything with purity of intention.

10. Be totally honorable and righteous.

11. Accept suffering with love.

12. Love Christ selflessly and with complete surrender.

13. Respond faithfully to the grace of God.

14. Live in Christ and only for Him.

BRIEF COMMENTARY ON THE FOURTEEN RULES

1. To be humble is to acknowledge the truth, to acknowledge who we truly are and how we stand before the justice of God. It means to put aside the magnifying glass of our pride and see our true worth clearly. Only then can we see our faults and limitations, our worst tendencies, our inability to do good, our absolute need for God and our need to be saved by him. This means to accept our spiritual poverty and merit the essential beatitude: "Blessed are the poor in spirit, for theirs is the kingdom of heaven" (Mt 5:3).

But it is not so hard to be humble before God; it just takes a little bit of common sense. The hard part is how to behave toward others in such a way as not to negate our promises to God through our conduct toward our brother or sister.

2. Let's be honest with each other. We have to admit that chastity is a virtue that is very difficult to practice. Everything begins with the stimulus we receive from the environment: on the street, in the movies, on television, in our interactions with others. As a result of these enticements, our minds begin to wander: our memories, our imagination, our desires. And all of this stimulates our bodily sexual desires and our natural responses.

If we want to be chaste according to our state in life, we need to be careful about what external stimulus we subject ourselves to.

We need to carefully guard our thoughts and understand how our body functions.

This is what is required by this second rule, because without chastity, we cannot grow in our spiritual life.

3. To be a person of prayer does not mean that you pray a lot of prayers, but rather, that you maintain a loving awareness of the presence of God, who is always with us and in us. This affectionate attention does not need words; it is a habit of frequently remembering that God constantly loves us as we put ourselves under his tender gaze.

To be a person of prayer also means to daily dedicate some time expressly to pray, to praise, to adore, to give thanks, to ask for forgiveness, to meditate, to love.

In the Spirituality of the Cross, to be a person of prayer also means to offer Jesus to the Father and to offer ourselves with the Son for the good of all people and to do this in union with Mary.

4. Everybody wants to make a good impression, to be seen in a good light, to let others see our merits so they may approve of us; we want them to hold us in esteem and applaud us. We would like to have an important position, to have authority, to give orders and even to be famous, if possible.

But all this fills our hearts with thoughts and concerns of ourselves and leaves no room for God. All this impedes us from searching for God's glory and seeking the good of others. All this is a source of anxiety, of envy and of ambitions that will rob us of our peace; and peace is an indispensable condition for uniting ourselves to God. For this reason, the fourth rule leads us to practice the modesty and the most profound humility of Christ.

5. Evangelical poverty works to free us from the bonds that come from the love of money and the attachment to material things.

For people who are actually poor, to follow Jesus in his

poverty means not having an ambition to be rich. It means to love your poverty, because it leads to spiritual freedom.

For people in the middle or upper class, evangelical poverty means to not attach your heart to your possessions, but rather to consider yourself an administrator in charge of what actually belongs to God. This means to understand that we do not own things and we take care of what has been given us as the true Owner wills it, that is, on behalf of those most in need (Mt 25:34-35).

6. In the final analysis, there are only two rivals who will contest the throne that exists in your heart: God and you yourself. Egoism leads us to live just for ourselves and to establish ourselves as the center of the small world that surrounds us: our family, our friends, the community we live in, etc.

But Jesus cautions us that unless we forget ourselves, we cannot be his disciples; if we wish to preserve our lives, we must lose our lives (Mt 10:39; Lk 14:26).

In summary, what you are lacking of God is exactly what you have in excess of yourself.

7. The same thing happens with earthly affections as in the case with earthly riches. The bad thing is not in having these affections, but rather in bonding so much to them that they deny us the freedom to experience God's love "above all things." Human affections will not disturb our love for God as long as they do not lead us to possessiveness.

On the other hand, there is such a thing as illegitimate affections that oppose the will of God, and these we must always avoid.

8. The love of the Mother of Christ is not something that is attainable on our own. It is a gift from God. But God will always give this gift to those who sincerely seek to live his plan, which is our salvation in Christ. In this rule, if we already have a love for Mary, we are asked to practice it more and more; if we do not have it yet, we

are asked to open ourselves to receive this grace, this marvelous gift.

9. Even our good works may be tainted with secondary intentions. We do things for God, but in a certain manner, we also do them for ourselves. The almsgiving, the penance, the prayer, the preaching, the good works, the apostolate... In all of this, there could be a residual vanity which tarnishes our love for God. A pure intention is like pure silver: it will not allow alloying with the presence of secondary intentions. This is what the ninth rule asks of us (read Mt 6:1-6).

10. There are many who call themselves good Christians and they see themselves almost as virtuous as saints. But they tell lies. They may steal small items; or they don't return borrowed items to their rightful owners; or they take part in shady business deals and in short, they disregard truth and honor, which are virtues practiced not only by good Christians, but even by good pagans. These are basic and fundamental practices; unfortunately, they have become difficult to uphold, because corruption has invaded our society to the point that no one wants to be an exception to the rule.

But God is Truth itself and Love itself. If you lie or defraud others, you are not with God and he is not with you.

11. In the Mass, we distinguish between the Offertory and the Consecration. First, we offer bread and wine; then Christ makes them his; these disappear, and only Christ remains. In the Spirituality of the Cross, we live our offertory when we offer ourselves to the Father together with Christ. But we live our consecration when God takes us at our word. The hour of trial and the hour of suffering are at hand, and we must then say: "Yes, Lord, this is my body and this is my blood and here is my life, all of my being, my possessions, my family and everything that I am and everything that I have."

In this rule, we are asked to daily practice our surrender as victims in small matters, to prepare us to be faithful when "our hour"– our moment of truth – finally arrives.

12. Selfless love is the only true love, and it is more rare than gold. Our initial love for God is filled with our own self-interest. St. Teresa of Avila tells us that in the first twenty years of her religious life, she had a "marriage of convenience." And if this is what happens with the great saints, what can we expect? This rule asks us to analyze deeply just how much our love for God is truly selfless, and to purify what is not by means of a total abandonment to his will.

13. The basic difference between the saints and us is that they responded fully to the grace of God, and we do not. They gave of themselves in complete surrender and with utmost enthusiasm, and they were radical. We are lazy, apathetic in spiritual matters, and miserly with God. God gives to us generously. God wants us to be saints. But we do not respond to his love, to his gifts, or to his mercy. This rule asks us to correct our ways, to wake up, and to imitate the saints.

14. The last rule asks us to convert our lives into one continuous Communion. It invites us to participation, even if only in a small way, in the grace of the mystical incarnation. It invites us to love Christ so completely and firmly that we truly deserve the fulfillment of his promise to us: "Whoever loves me will keep my word and my Father will love him and we will come and make our dwelling with him" (Jn 14:23).

Books on the Spirituality of the Cross available in English

Concepcion Cabrera de Armida
- Seasons of the Soul
- Before the Altar
- Holy Hours
- Our Lady of Solitude
- A Mother's Letters
- Roses and Thorns
- I am, Meditations on the Gospel
- What Jesus is Like
- Loving with the Holy Spirit
- To be Jesus Crucified
- Under the Gaze of the Father

Mons. Luis Ma. Martínez, Archbishop México
- The Sanctifier
- The True Devotion to the Holy Spirit
- Spread your Wings
- Meditations for Christmas

By Other Authors
- Conchita, A Mother's Spiritual Diary, Fr. M. M. Philipon O.P.
- Conchita a Modern Mystic, Fr. M.M. Philipon O.P.
- Transforming Prayer for Pilgrims, Mons. Gustavo Garcia Siller, M.Sp.S. Archbishop of San Antonio, TX
- Conchita's Spiritual Journey, Fr. Ignacio Navarro, M.Sp.S.
- Irresistibly Drawn to the Eucharist, Fr. Juan Gutierrez, M.Sp.S.
- Mystical Incarnation in Concepción Cabrera de Armida, Sr. Laura Linares, rcscj
- Mystical Incarnation – Fr. Bernardo Olivera, ocso
- A Glorious Cross, Sr. Dolores Icaza rcscj
- You Belong to the Church, Sr. Elzbieta Sadowska, rcscj
- This Beautiful Cross, Sr. Elzbieta Sadowska, rcscj
- The Priesthood of Christ, Msgr. Juan Esquerda Bifet

- Risking the Future, Life and Spirituality of Fr. Felix of Jesus Rougier, M.Sp.S., by Fr. Ricardo Zimbron, M.Sp.S.
- The Message of the Cross, Fr. Roberto de la Rosa, M.Sp.S.
- I Was Baptized with the Name of Maria Concepcion, Maria Guadalupe Labarthe,rcscj
- Spiritual Direction According to the Simple Plan, Fr. Roberto de la Rosa, M.Sp.S.

FAVORS AND GRACES RECEIVED
BY THE INTERCESSION OF CONCHITA MAY BE SENT TO

Sisters of the Cross of the Sacred Heart of Jesus
1320 Maze Boulevard
Modesto, CA, 95351
USA
email: sistersofthecross@yahoo.com

My dear reader, before you close this book, I want to give you two pieces of advice. The first is this, after some time reread this book at least one more time. It was good for me to write this book, but it did me even more good to go over it, correcting the words, revising the book over and over. I believe that the first time we read this, we are captivated by the narrative and anecdotal aspect of Conchita's life. But on the second reading, one can capture the real substance of her works, and little by little, a person can perceive the distinct and multiple teachings contained in this book from the beginning to the end. The first reading is done hurriedly. But on the second reading, one proceeds slowly, reflecting on each concept.

And here is my second piece of advice: If you know someone who is suffering in his or her body or soul, give that person this book as a gift, because there are many crosses that wound excessively. This is so, because some people do not know how to carry them. There is much suffering that is wasted. There is much pain that should be a blessing, but instead it is nothing more than a cry in the desert that gets lost.

But in sharing the spirituality of Christ as Priest and Victim, you will give light and comfort to someone who suffers; you will offer that person what he or she needs to turn this suffering into a pathway to holiness.

If you desire to be a member of one of the Works of the Cross, ask for information at one of the churches of the Missionaries of the Holy Spirit or in a convent of the Sisters of the Cross of the Sacred Heart of Jesus.

Sisters of the Cross

of the Sacred Heart of Jesus

1320 Maze Blvd.

Modesto, CA 95351   USA

Telephone: 1-209-526-3525

Christ the Priest Provincial House

39085 NW Harrington Rd

Banks, OR 97106   USA

Telephone: 1-503-324-2492

https://religiosasdelacruz.wordpress.
com/nuestros-libros//
modesto01diffusion@live.com